A Journey Towards Peaceful Living

by

Fred W. Abrahamson

A Journey Towards Peaceful Living

ISBN 978-0-615-51325-6 softcover
978-0-615-51530-4 hardcover

Printed in the United States of America

Dedication

This book is dedicated to my sons, their wives, and my grandchildren. May the Lord bless and keep them all safe.

Also to my sisters: Jeanne, who always has kept me in her prayers, for me to find my way in troubling times. I am grateful for her tenacity. I can only hope to have learned some of the lessons that I was afforded me along the way. And my sister Eileen, who has quietly wished me well and showed me love, compassion and patience. She, however, refers to me as her "bother," instead of brother. I do love them both dearly. And only hope that I can be of any assistance to them in their times of need.

I am also grateful for my loving parents, who have passed on. Although they are no longer on this earth, they are still very much with me in spirit.

I am very blessed to have so many people come into my life at the absolutely right times. They have brought so many positive influences and valuable lessons to learn.

My process of becoming more aware, striving for a higher level of consciousness, has started and is continually ongoing. This journey is not about the destination, it's about the process of trusting along the way. There is no turning back, as we can't turn back the hands of time, or hold back the tide. A prayer of gratitude goes out to each and every one of you for your help, support, and understanding. Thank you all, for you have deeply touched my life with your wonderful energy and awareness. I am eternally grateful.

Contents

Acknowledgments

I am truly grateful for all the help I have received in the process of writing this book. Without this loving help, the book would not have been possible. It is a compilation of things I have learned, through experience or through the guidance of others on their journeys. For me, the journey started about fourteen years ago, although the writing started taking shape only in 2009.

I would like to first acknowledge my parents, who are no longer with us here on earth. I lovingly think of you both often. As I think back now, they made a wonderful impact on my life with the fingerprints they left behind.

Special acknowledgment needs to be expressed to Toni Arland for reading and making constructive comments that have only helped to make this a better book—as well as for her allowing me to present some of the chapters in speeches to her Thursday class. Sandra Montgomery also spent time reading and offering suggestions to help with the flow of the chapters. Debbie Anderson, a long time friend, has always encouraged my personal growth, and she offered comments regarding various chapters. I finished the book with the support and encouragement of these three woman, along with unnamed others who have influenced the ebb and flow of these chapters. Thank you all for your patience, honesty, effort and time.

Bob Crow, both a personal friend and my hypnotherapist, led me through improvements in my public speaking—and my writing—styles.

My journey started when I attended personal growth classes sponsored by Newton Learning and the Wings organization. Not only did I attend these seminars, I also had an opportunity to assist in some small ways during some of them. I have been blessed to have met some wonderful loving people, some of whom I still stay in contact with.

Some of these friends are friends of a lifetime, for a lifetime. Thank you.

In the lessons I have learned along the way on this journey are numerous contributors who are unnamed, and yet have played essential roles in the development of my life and this book. Without their influences, this book would not be what it is today—or perhaps may not even been written.

I also am very grateful for the editing I received from Barbara Fifer; she put this book into the final form that you are now holding.

Special thanks to Paul and JoAnn White, who have allowed me to use their photograph from a trip to the Pacific Northwest coast as the basis for the front cover. And also to Linda Mc-Cray for her artistic talents in painting that watercolor, and designing the book cover.

Author's Note

This journey that we are all on is about just that—our own personal journey. And our destinations are always out there in the future. So this is a journey toward the realm of peaceful living. And you are your own architect. The most exciting point of this journey is that we get to embrace and enjoy each and every moment.

This book's subject matter was inspired by various books I have read. For a listing of some of those titles, please go to my web site, www. lifespeacefuljourneys.com/

Introduction

A new day dawns in our lives and we begin to become aware of our "being-ness." As well as the lives we touch and that in turn touch our own. This is not a narrow view, for it could expand to include the world.

For different people "the world" has different meanings, for some it's just the community or area in which they live, for others it's the state or nation and, for yet others, it is the world. And where do most of us actually live? Whether we are aware or not, the answer is within ourselves.

This is where we are challenged to reach our God-given potential. It is this energy that is within us all, that we manifest at different levels of our lives, and that at different times can in turn be projected out into this world, and our universe. Therefore, what is of the most importance for each of us to know? The answer is simply to "Know Thyself."

It has been said that wise people study other people, and those searching or reaching for enlightenment study themselves. We can all learn many valuable lessons by the study of other people. It allows us the opportunity to explore the decisions and paths of some incredibly wise and wonderfully talented individuals. Thereby, allowing us to understand their decision-making processes as well as studying the paths they have embarked upon.

Then we can begin to understand how some of their decisions have or could have impacted our lives. These lessons should never be discounted, because of their great value. Our challenge is in the search for understanding of other people's wisdom.

Ultimately, what is the real quest of our own personal journey? It is the study within our being, or sense of oneself, expressed as "thyself."

Why is that of any importance to us? Why not just drift through life aimlessly?

Because, at some point in time, we will realize we are all individually responsible for who we are—not our parents, not our spouses or other people. Yes, family, friends and other people have given us guidance, encouragement, love, and these too are important.

We, however, have molded ourselves to who we are, by the decisions we have made in our pasts, which could have been influenced by others in our lives, as well as our personal environments. We should also realize that we can make different decisions or choices moving forward into the future, which can make an enormous difference in our lives. Because our decisions right now affect our futures!

It is then important to remember, we have all entered this world alone and this is the way we shall leave. So it is up to us to contemplate the fingerprint we will all place on this world, when we do pass on to the next realm.

What will your fingerprint look like? Remember, it very possibly could be reflected in the lives you have touched by your thoughts, deeds and actions (either consciously or unconsciously), and how others will in turn go about touching future lives with their fingerprints in this act of living here on earth.

The more we begin to learn about ourselves, the more our awareness increases, and the better aligned we'll be to make good or better choices, "the right decisions," which will affect not only ourselves, but could also have an effect on those we touch.

What is the right decision or choice? It is a feeling within our being, which we intuitively sense "feels right" to our core beliefs.

How do we know if it really is the right decision? It may be a matter of trusting yourself as well as the process. Perhaps an easier way to explain this answer is to look at the converse. When we reach a decision and it is uncomfortable and causes unrest internally, we know it was an incorrect decision for us personally. But we are all "of choice," so we can re-choose.

Also, when we reach a decision, then we have the opportunity to "try it on." If we feel uncomfortable, the more aware we are, the better we'll start to know it intuitively. This sensing by intuition may take some practice, ways of calming ourselves and trusting the process. From the study of kinesiology we learn that the body doesn't lie.

Thus, by understanding the body's language by the ability to use our own muscles as indicators, we become better aware of our own conditions. When things are good within our bodies our muscles test strong; when our muscles test weak, something is misaligned within ourselves. In our daily lives, we tend to allow ourselves to get tied up and forget to listen to our bodies. Until something dramatic happens, like a heart attack or other serious event.

Maybe we could start or should start to listen more intently to ourselves, because our bodies are continually speaking to us, giving us signs and signals. If we become better at listening and start to recognize the smaller bumps in the road of our lives, perhaps we can forgo the heart attacks (so to speak) of life.

When a small incorrect choice is made we may have some choices: 1—re-choose; or, 2—ignore the signal. When we dismiss these internal feelings we tend to start a process of desensitizing ourselves. Remember these signals are warnings for us at some internal level.

Also, when this desensitizing process starts, it can then be easier to continue along its path, building resistance. That is, until we recognize a change must be made to preserve our life and its functions. So it is to our benefit to start to remove the walls that we have been so good at building up in the process of ignoring the signs.

Therefore this book offers the reader an opportunity to learn some or more about "thyself" for ourselves, if you choose. Then you will have an opportunity to embrace what you have learned. The option is entirely yours to choose, but it could allow you to make better choices through your own decision-making process.

Remember, there are no mistakes in life, only lessons. The word mistake can be broken down to "miss take," so when we make a "miss take," now we know we can "re-take" or "re-choose." Because the "miss," as in the case when an archer misses his target, allows him to try again with another shot. This can also be the case when we have a "miss" by the decision we made and have not hit our target, now we can try again, we can re-choose.

Many years ago, in an interview with Thomas Edison, the interviewer asked Mr. Edison about all the failures he had encountered in the discovery of the electric light. His answer was, and I'm paraphrasing here, these were not failures, they were however lessons in how *not* to make the electric light.

As I look back upon my own life's journey, I can see that, in my younger years, I made some decisions which were other than good or right for me personally. During these times I did not recognize them as mistakes, just as plain decisions.

As I grew older, I came to recognize them as mistakes. Some were small, some large, some were incredibly stupid. Now, as I look back, I have come to the realization that they were all lessons. For which I am grateful, because they have offered me some wonderful opportunities and lessons to grow as a person. For me, this has come to be, mainly because of my eagerness to increase my personal awareness, the process of "know thyself."

Every lesson has a purpose and every setback in life has its set of lessons. As in the case of Thomas Edison, he didn't view wrong decisions as failures because they offered him lessons. The realization here is for our personal, professional and spiritual internal growth. This is an opportunity or chance for internal exploration; past experiences can be wonderful teachers, so don't look at things in the past and hold them in regret. Look at these "experiential lessons" as offering valuable rewards and opportunities for growth.

Our life's journey will ultimately unfold by the decisions we make. Our choices are therefore and always have been ours alone to make, or to re-choose.

We can all be on this exciting new frontier of self-exploration. That is, if we choose to continue to move forward. The journey is to "know thyself." Let the journey begin! May there be blessing to all; enjoy the journey and/or process.

Personal notes...

Personal notes...

The Journey

On this journey which has been my life I have come to realize how fortunate and blessed I have been all these years.

As with most of us I was born at a very young age. And it was at home not in a hospital. The city is in the upper Midwest. The original name came from the Potawatomi Indians and is pronounced *Chick-Ah-Goo-Ah*, its meaning "wild onions." That city is now called *Chicago*.

Growing up, I had loving parents and three older sisters. My dad worked long hours to provide for his family. My mom had a full-time job taking care of us kids.

As I got older, mom took a part-time job, while I was in school. Mom was a wonderful cook and they both did the best they could for us kids. Dad was a handyman around the house, as you had to be during those years; in my eyes, he could do anything. This was in the late Forties and early Fifties.

My two oldest sisters were married by the time I was ten. The youngest daughter in the family, Eileen, the one closest to my age, now refers to me as her *bother* instead of her brother. The middle sister, Jeanne, married Herb, who at one point in time started calling me Derf; Derf is Fred spelled backwards. I did NOT consider this a term of endearment. He thought it was funny, I didn't. Oh well, I was just a kid at the time.

Three major events happened in my life as I moved through youth to becoming an adult. These allowed me to understand and realize that I have the ability to fulfill my life's dreams. Yet I didn't fully understand this until years later, when I was of course older. As I look back now it seems to have been a kind of intuitive knowing.

I would be foolish however to think that these three major events happened only with my intervention. Therefore I sincerely believe that a power far greater than I guided the right people to enter my life at exactly the right time.

Either seen or unseen! Why? Because there are no accidents.

Have you ever felt that the right things just fall into place, or have you ever asked yourself why you are so lucky? Now perhaps you may have experienced the converse to the above statement. At those times nothing seems to be going your way. You may even ask yourself, what did I do, to deserve this?

Back to my three special events, which are:

1. Becoming an Eagle Scout, at the age of fifteen. For me it was an ideal time in my life. We lived in the country on a lake in Central Florida. I learned to swim, camp and a host of other things a young scout is eager to master. On this trail to becoming an Eagle Scout.

2. Receiving my bachelor's degree in Electrical Engineering Technology from DeVry. After finishing high school, I really didn't know if I wanted to go to college or not. I had a love of electronics and was a ham radio operator while in high school.

My parents encouraged that I continue my education. DeVry was a good choice for me, as they offered an associate degree in Electronics. While at DeVry I got far better grades than I did in high school, and really enjoyed what I was learning.

After completing their program I accepted a position at Xerox in Webster, New York. Then after a couple of years I returned to the Chicago area and accepted a position at Motorola. I was young and single, so guess what happened next? I got a letter from Uncle Sam. So off to the U.S. Army I went.

After serving my two years I returned home and back to work at Motorola. Although, the only position now available in the same lab where I had worked was that of working nights, the second shift. Also at about the same time I learned that DeVry now offered a bachelor's degree. And with my credits from the associate's degree I only had about a year to go to complete my BSEE. This turn of events allowed me to go to school full time during the days and work full time at Motorola on second shift.

3. After working for Motorola for about ten years I accepted a job offer from a manufacturer's representative company in the area. It was in high technology sales of vacuum technology and semiconductors, as well as other related technologies.

I started as their service manager then a couple of years later went into sales, working there about eight years; this allowed me to learn a great deal about the business, from a sales point of view as well as in the aspects of running a business. These two job experiences, in turn, led to my starting my own business over twenty-five years ago.

These events have gotten me to where I am today professionally.

Looking back now, I think perhaps the greatest series of events started in motion several months after a personal tragedy, which was a very low point in my life. That was my second divorce. Running a business requires a lot of time and attention. Perhaps the old adage is true: too much work can lead to personal tragedies. I know now that I didn't always have my priorities set correctly.

From this low point, with the help and encouragement of friends, I started a quest for my own personal growth. Such growth is a journey within ourselves.

We have all heard the words "know thyself." How these words ring so true! Can this journey be shared? Absolutely! It's all a matter of where you are, as well as the willingness, and openness of those you choose to share your life with, as well as your inner self.

Shortly after starting this quest, I attended a couple of personal growth seminars. At one three-day seminar, during the second day we were all given an assignment. Each of us was to write our own personal life's vision statement. All the statements varied, as did the individuals. I would like to share mine with you at this time:

I Am a Sincere, Faithful, Compassionate Man, Living My Life in Joy.

So, where am I? Who am I? I believe that I am open to life. There has been such an abundance of loving, caring, nurturing people who have entered my life. Some only for a short time, to perhaps show or teach me some lesson(s)! Others stayed longer, either as teachers or as students. Our job here on earth is that of either teacher or student, and those roles can change in a heartbeat.

I like to think of my life as a wonderful positive journey. Mainly because, I choose NOT to entertain any negative thought processes. I have been blessed in countless ways. These blessings allow me the opportunity to share all that I have learned with others. This too is a personal choice. I choose to take nothing for granted. I am grateful for the air that I breathe, and all that I have. My last blessing is for the wonderful positive energy from you the reader of my humble little book, which would not have been possible without your involvement.

Personal notes...

Personal notes...

Energy

I'd like to start by giving you a couple of definitions of the word energy.

Energy—the strength and vitality required to sustain physical or mental activities.

Energy—always moving, never stops, always in motion, can't be suppressed or repressed.

When we think of LIFE—it's much the same as energy, always moving, never stops; well, perhaps it stops at death—or does it? If we exchange the word *life* with the word *spirit*—it never dies! A discussion on spirit would require a person far more knowledgeable and educated than I. But I do, however, believe we are all made up of energy.

Therefore, regarding energy, a person would

be foolish to attempt to restrict the flow of energy. If the universe is composed of a pure energy or perhaps made up of several energy fields of different magnitudes, thus we are in or part of this wonderful energy field. Yet we cannot hold energy, nor can we see energy, we can only enjoy sensing this energy as it flows through us.

Let's look at energy within humans; it basically falls into two categories—positive and negative. Most people want positive energy. Sometimes that presents a challenge, particularly when we feel stuck in some negative situation.

Whenever we're in a funk, feeling down or negative, it may seem an impossible task to move positively. Although all it takes is our willingness to allow just one small positive movement in our energy. Once the first step is taken the subsequent steps may become easier.

A few year ago, I read a volume in Masaru Emoto's book series, *Messages from Water*. As his study of water structures developed, he learned about the effects of various energy fields and environments.

It's very interesting in that he has captured different energy levels in water with pictures of the structures like droplets and crystals within different water samples. In them, you can plainly see the effect of environments, as well as energy fields.

Regarding energy, let's use a glass of water to understand how energy can flow or not flow. We can easily see that once the glass is full of water, no more water can be added (thus there is no flow of energy). If you attempt to add more water, it will flow out and over the containing glass. However, if we desire more energy (water in this case) we would need to give away some of this water, thus allowing more room for additional water (or energy) to be added.

Now if we look at the energy of life (which we all have) flowing through us, and we try to hold on to this energy, what do you think happens? It will always flow or move on its own. Remember, energy can't be repressed or suppressed in our lives, and all we have is this one moment of time to enjoy that particular moment of energy. Then we'll get the next moment, and so forth and so on.

Life is to be lived moment to moment and all the moments can and should be embraced. These moments compose our lives. Eckhart Tolle wrote a book titled *The Power of Now*, which teaches focusing on the "now," because that is all we really have anyway. The past is past, the future hasn't yet arrived, therefore we might want to consider the value in embracing the now.

Energy is universal—it's everywhere, and I mean everywhere! We each are composed of energy and therefore can add our own part of energy to this universal energy field. When we come together with others who share the same energy level we can get stronger.

Thus, being mindful, we should take care, as it could work both negatively as well as positively.

A prime and positive example of this universal energy field came about was a result of one of the United States' worse disasters, the 9-11 attacks. Some might say that there were a lot of thoughts of revenge—yes of course there were. Commendably, there were also many thoughts of compassion to those who were lost and all those left behind by loved ones and friends.

This movement of compassion from all around the world united people in a positive, compassionate energy field. This type of union has been seen time and time again; even though the resulting positive energy field effects can't easily be explained, they have occurred nonetheless.

We could also cite events like the Indian

Ocean tsunami of 2004 or even the Atlantic's hurricane Katrina in 2005. These tragedies were made both by man and by nature.

This resulting energy effect could also be called by another term—an elevated level of human consciousness. Any and all levels of consciousness carry with them some degree of energy.

In the book *Power vs. Force*, David R. Hawkins does an excellent job of explaining those different levels in regard to energy. He uses a logarithmic scale to describe energy levels. It starts at 20 and goes up to 1000.

At the upper level of the scale we have Enlightenment, and at the lower end we have Shame. One is very positive, the other very negative. Hawkins also has words that describe different energy levels as well as their corresponding emotional words.

Let me give you a couple of examples: at 20 we have Shame, which is emotionally Humiliation, and at 700 to 1000 we have Enlightenment which is emotionally Ineffable. Has anyone been at the level 1000? Yes—Jesus. There have been and are others who reached Enlightenment as well, like Mother Teresa and Gandhi, just to name two.

At what level do we move from Negative to Positive? The answer is—level 200! Let's look at two people who operated on different sides of the 200 level, at the same period in time. One is Adolf Hitler—who, Hawkins says, generally operated at 100 to 150 or lower; the other, Winston Churchill, was significantly above the 200 level.

All levels of human consciousness directly relates to energy levels. Allow me to tell you a few from *Power vs. Force*:

20	Shame	Humiliation
100	Fear	Anxiety
150	Anger	Hate
200	Courage	Affirmation
350	Acceptance	Forgiveness
500	Love	Reverence
700–1000	Enlightenment	Ineffable

Now you may be wondering, what does the word "ineffable" mean? It is "incapable of being described or expressed in words."

We can then also think of the old saying "mind over matter"—is it true or untrue? I happen to believe that there is more substance to matter than simply meets the eye. Or, perhaps better stated, meets the mind.

Now if we are all part of this universal energy field, perhaps there really is some type of "universal cosmic consciousness." Then we, as humans beings, with our own minds can contribute to the positive-ness this energy consciousness, if we so choose.

Why would a person choose not to be a positive influence in this universal energy? Maybe they choose to not contribute because of their level of energy or the lack thereof. If a person feels they can make no difference they tend to not make an attempt to contribute.

Another subtle way of not having positive energy would be to withhold or restrict the flow of energy. This could be found in the restrictiveness of being at odds with another person, to the point of expending energy to wish harm to befall another. Which, in my view, is a waste of our valuable energy.

Let me give you an example of such restrictiveness: say that you, as a person, have an unkind thought toward another person. This thought could be anything that has caused some internal level of unrest or *un-peacefulness*.

Keep in mind that the other person might not even be aware of your internal struggle and they most certainly won't be affected by it. It could start as something small, and the person may be completely unaware. As that person moves forward in their day they may see and be attached to other signs of unrest. Thus the energy (negative or positive) can have a building effect.

Could this affect others? When a person is involved with others on a daily basis, absolutely! And then when the person's day is going in a downward spiral they may think back and say, how did this whole mess get started anyway?

It started with one small restriction of your energy, or attempting to hold onto something that was perceived as negative energy or as a negative thought.

Then how do we correct such a state? Simply by changing to a positive thought and allowing the flow of positive energy to replace this negative effect.

You may say "How do I get a positive thought?" How about this for an example: when you see a baby laugh or giggle, how can you have any thoughts other than LOVE, which is very positive? That's how it can start. Basically by the giving away one simple, small positive thought of energy to another person, followed by another and another, and so forth and so on.

We may have heard of the statement

"What you perceive you receive and you will attract that which you give away." So what do you want?

Will we, as humans, stumble and fall back or regress, from time to time? The answer is found in the saying "We are only human." And when we are *aware* we can re-choose and let the energy flow positively again.

Think of energy flowing like water through an unrestricted garden hose. Now, if we allow ourselves to be viewed as personal energy portals, we need to have energy flow through us individually. Thus this life-giving energy must be allowed to flow through our beings. That is, if we do not restrict the flow, by attempting to hold on to something that can't be held in the first place.

As humans we would all like to hold on to the good times, and we can—they're called memories. We should all keep the good memories in our minds and let go of all other stuff, especially anything negative.

There is a difference in having a wonderful memory and attempting to relive a good memory of the past. There lies the challenge! Perhaps you or someone you know feels enslaved to only the negative thoughts of the past. Who made that decision or that choice? You guessed it, the individual did.

A close friend of mine, Debbie, once said to me, "When you are aware of something that doesn't seem or feel quite right, remember you are human and say 'Oh, you silly human,' and re-choose." With the lightness and gentleness of her statement, she expressed allowing forgiveness and moving on to positive ground.

When a person is intertwined in the realm of negative thoughts, choosing positivity may not seem easy. But it can, however, start with the smallest positive change in any life and it starts with the simple act of re-choosing. Keep in mind I said "start" but know that the rest of the results are in your hands.

All change in perspective may take time, by allowing the flow of positive energy into your life. By this simple act you are raising your consciousness as well as the consciousness of the universe, one mind at a time.

We could even think of this energy as brain energy, which can have an effect on the universe and can even be referred to as brain energy radiation. Or how about this, thought-emissions (moving outward) of thought energy?

How could this work in our daily lives? I

think it could incredibility enhance our going forward. This could foster a change in the entire paradigm of conventional thinking. Some of the things that have been present in our lives have been in the form of delusions, some from ourselves. Yet others have been planted in our minds by other people.

Some of these misperceptions are, or could be, the result of closed-mindedness. Nonetheless, sometimes it may be worth considering a new and/or higher path. It's now all in your hands, be mindful of your energy levels.

Here is a notable quote:

Our deepest fear is not that we are inadequate. Our deepest fear is that we are powerful beyond measure. It is our light, not our darkness, that most frightens us. We ask ourselves, who am I to be brilliant, gorgeous, talented, and fabulous? Actually who are you not to be? You are a child of God. Your playing small doesn't serve the world. There's nothing enlightened about shrinking so that other people won't feel insecure around you. We were born to manifest the glory of God within us; it's in everyone. And as we let our own light shine, we unconsciously give other people

permission to do the same. As we're liber-
ated from our fear, our presence automati-
cally liberates others.
                    —Marianne Williamson

Personal notes...

Personal notes...

Who Said I'm Resisting?!

How calming our lives could be if we were to allow ourselves peacefulness by not resisting the flow and ebb of life! But, do you even realize when you are resisting?

While we look at resistance or non-resistance, try viewing it as I do, from my background in electrical engineering.

From an electronics point of view, resistance measures how much a wire or other entity naturally impedes or resists the flow of electric current through it. Translating that to life, think of resistance as fighting the flow of the experiences or the energy of life as it comes our way.

How do people resist? In some very basic ways—like not yielding to or accepting something different for themselves. Let me give you a few general examples: new foods, clothing, activities, points of view, or interests. Resistance is not yielding, accepting or even temporarily going along with something (or anything) new and different.

Let's take foods as an example. Here's one of my personal resistances: head cheese! Have you ever tried that stuff? Well, my personal description would be "Yuk!" The first and only time I tried head cheese, I was married and we were in a grocery store. The staff, bless their hearts, were offering samples. My wife said "Try it, it's good," so I tried it. Up to the point of putting head cheese in my mouth, I was in non-resistance. After tasting it, I couldn't find a place to spit that stuff out of my mouth fast enough. Trust me, I even thought about putting it behind a can of peas or something. Do you know what head cheese is made of? I don't want to!

The point is, though, that when I had the opportunity to try something new, I chose to try it. At that point I was in non-resistance. When given an opportunity, we all should consider trying something new so we will know whether we like it or not. Even though my reaction to head cheese is negative, many people do enjoy it, and that is just fine.

Another personal example of food is what my boys consider "strange food," and that's raw fish, which I rather enjoy, although they would never let it pass their lips. Now, my grandson will eat sushi, as will one of my daughters-in-law. See, it all really is our own personal choice.

With these examples it shows that we can all have different reactions to something new and different, something other than normal from our personal perspectives. And it's always okay to choose different paths when presented with something unfamiliar. There will always be opportunities to explore things that are new and different if we choose to do so. Sometimes our personal growth happens when we say YES and explore the unknown.

Keep in mind that if you don't try something, you may never really know what it's like to experience whatever opportunity was presented to you. Now, a person should of course look for any real danger in any opportunity. What potential risk is involved, and could it be harmful to you or to other people? You are free to choose "no" and forgo this opportunity, remembering that this is your personal choice. It's okay to have chosen to close the door to that particular opportunity for yourself; just remember that it was your choice. But for all the things that are not dangerous, look back at the things that you *didn't* say no to in your life so far. And the enjoyment you experienced, and or the lessons you learned. There lie some of the real opportunities of the adventure in life; it's with these new experiences.

Another thing about saying NO to someone or something is that it might just be an ingrained response. Why would anyone always say no as a first response? Because the "new" doesn't feels "normal" or perhaps even because the individual feels threatened or afraid! Like being afraid of making a commitment, and then feeling stuck with your decision. Remember you can always re-choose.

Fear could be because the outcome is indeterminable. Maybe we're stuck in a "no" mode, and resistance offers some perceived comfort. Could it be the ego just waiting to be involved and rearing its head in defiance? Whatever the case, this resistance triggers something within us to react in a form of non-compliance or resistance, and in whatever form it may take for a particular situation.

If fear sounds like the basic form of your resistance, how could this be resolved? You might want to read the book titled *Feel the Fear and Do It Anyway* by Susan Jeffers. Can your fear be eliminated? What's really important is how a person deals with fear. It has been said that fear is something a person can't go around, it must be gone through. But, if resistance is a form of fear, how do we go through something that we are afraid to confront? Once the particular fear can be viewed as a non-fear or, better stated, as non-threatening, then there may be little or no resistance.

Where did our predisposed notion of resistance come from? Well, it all starts in our minds. How did something like this enter our minds? Basically we let it in. It could have been placed there by loved ones, perhaps during our early years, also by friends, relatives and colleagues or by ourselves with the decisions we have made. And, yes, with the help and encouragement of the ever-present ego! The power of the mind is, for the most part, limited only by the user (yourself).

When we think of all that we live with or utilize, other than that found in nature, it's amazing. All these things started as a thought in someone's mind. And those thoughts brought about inventions, which came from the attention that people gave to their intentions. They were in non-resistance to their dreams and aspirations.

Such dreams can also been defined as "passions." So maybe we should "Mind our own business," and pay good attention to the thoughts we allow into our minds. This can and should be our main business, along with nourishing those new thoughts and ideas.

Are there times when resistance can serve us? Absolutely! Some resistances can keep us safe. It's like making a decision on right or wrong. By resisting making a poor decision, we have done the right thing. Ah, you may say, what is this right thing or decision?

In most cases you will know it intuitively, by the state of peacefulness or the lack of peacefulness, thus unrest, within our beings. With our increased awareness it could be sensed by our hearts, for example. In most cases we should all resist non-truths or harmful temptations. Haven't we all heard the saying "The devil made me do it!" My answer is, "Well, who do you think made that choice?"

When we act in non-resistance, we allow things to happen, with a simple yes. Whereas nothing happens when we say no and close off those channels of opportunities.

We could also look at this as life's energy that we're allowing to flow through us by not attempting to refuse or *resist* it. Probably one of the reasons a person wants to stay stuck in resistance is because they don't want to let go of a beautiful and wonderful moment or experience. Sometimes even the converse is true, with a negative event that has been experienced. If a person is carrying around negativity from past events, it can take its toll. Then we should consider letting go of these past thoughts, which no longer serve our well being. Here is an expression to consider: "If the horse is dead, get off of it!"

We need to view all our past lessons with loving thoughts, for they have served to show or teach us something. They helped make us who we are right NOW, as we brought ourselves to this very moment in time by the decisions we have made.

But why would anyone want to carry around unpleasant memories? Perhaps it's because they made those personal choices, either consciously or unconsciously! If we are building memories that always reside in our past, why not just remember the good stuff? Because other than good, memories really have no value.

What we put in our minds is a choice, so choose wisely, and choose positive memories that have the effect of positive, life-evolving energy. Negative thoughts are destructive and debilitating to our energy, so release them and let them go. Again, when the horse is dead get off of it. And continue on with the positivity of your life.

This doesn't mean we can just wipe out the negative memories, nor should we. Experiences that have been negative in the past allow us to make better decisions in the future. That is, if we have learned our lessons! If not, we will get another opportunity to learn that particular lesson again. Because the lessons will keep returning until we stop resisting and learn the lessons that are there to be learned.

When we resist, we block the flow of energy, which is our life force. So when an issue or situation arises and you feel resistance to whatever it is, examine it. Ask yourself, Why and what am I resisting? This is the path towards developing awareness to allow you to start clearing the lens through which you view your life and your different situations.

Then you can look at this journey through life and say, "Sometimes my life's up and sometimes my life's down." When we're up, we can be very up, and when we're down—no one wants to join us, at those deep and dark depths. Do you really want to be around someone in a bad mood, or who's having a bad day? Hey, would YOU really want to be around YOU, when you're down and in an ugly mood? Of course not, who wants to subject themselves to that environment? It's a negative energy field, so to speak.

In summary, the energy of life is in constant motion, therefore we should allow it to flow through us, without restrictions or resistance. And we can all be thankful, for it allows faith and hope to enter our lives.

I was attending a board meeting a few years back and there was a group of about six people opposed to some motions to be voted on. At first, I was seated next to this group, but the negative energy was so powerful that I needed to move. This was something I just sensed, but once I moved, I felt a whole lot better.

For me it was about being aware and acknowledging my internal signs. In this case, was my resistance to this negative energy a good thing? Yes! And I was taking care of myself, my well being.

When a situation arises, think: "If *I* say NO,

am I resisting, and if so, for what reasons? What do I *lose* or *gain* by saying NO?" Sometimes a particular situation might offer a wonderful experience, only for you. You are choosing experiencing or not experiencing, adding to your life or restricting your life. If, however, you were to say *"Yes"* and move forward, and it doesn't work out to your liking, remember you are of choice, so you can re-choose.

After all, what happens when you resist by not allowing something, anything, to happen, is that you gain no growth through the particular experience. And who is the person most likely to really be affected? You guessed it! You made the personal decision, so it's up to you, yourself, to make the next choice! Knowing you can "re-choose" is a powerful lesson, and it's a gift of awareness.

A point to remember about resisting is: *What we resist, persists*, especially if life is offering us a lesson that we *need* to learn.

Personal notes...

*P*ersonal notes...

An Open Heart

When and only when you have opened your own heart will you have the ability to touch and open the hearts of others. It is within the heart we find this quiet simplicity, for the heart does not want to complicate issues. It just wants to offer love. This immense power of simplicity should never be overlooked or disregarded.

The opening of a heart and the offering of love require openness without any expectations or motives. How do we get to that point? It is with using love as the cornerstone of this, our foundation.

Once we have love in place, the rest of our personal life's construction can proceed with a smoothness and ease that we may have never felt in the past. It is worth remembering that this feeling can be ours at any time we choose. It is a matter of quieting ourselves, to allow this inner peacefulness to wash over our bodies, minds and spiritual selves.

What is the biggest obstacle to an open heart? Perhaps it's forgiveness! Let's look at a closed heart. In this process of closing our heart towards others we, in turn, only do harm to ourselves. Some might think that by closing off and not offering love to another we are stronger or perhaps more powerful. That is only the ego speaking. However, in the process of not allowing any love out to another person, we have also closed ourselves off from any love being received.

This "valve," so to speak, is not a one-way valve. Whatever flows out is directly proportional to what has the opportunity to flow in.

Is anyone a winner with this type of restriction, or does anyone come out victorious? Absolutely not, everyone involved in such actions loses. An unopened heart restricts the opportunity for that heart to expand through love.

Why would a person choose a path such as this? There could be a multitude of reasons. Along with not forgiving, we could also have selfishness, where life is all about our own selves, not about other people. It makes no difference where the other person's heart is at this very moment, the only real concern is where your heart is.

With this changing of our perspective, we have the opportunity to offer love. The offering of love, will always—all-ways—alter an issue or situation and even has the potential to impact another person's view or prospective. Yet the largest benefits are the blessings and healing power we have offered ourselves.

As we are all on our own personal journeys upon this earth, it would be beneficial to ourselves and others to offer only heartfelt love. By this simple act of freely giving love, we will receive in abundance all that is in our destiny.

With our hearts open and full of love, there can be no room for un-loving thoughts. Our minds can only process one thought at a time. If you think I'm kidding, try giving someone your heart-felt love and being hateful, angry or judgmental to that same person at the same time. It is our choice, to act either as givers, or withholders. Which would you choose? Where would you find peace?

In the process of opening our hearts, the

ultimate benefit is to offer forgiveness to ourselves. Looking at this open-heart process, as we begin to purge unhealthy thoughts from our minds, we begin to add a new level of fullness to our lives. Can this purging be completely accomplished? Maybe yes, maybe no, for the ego will always give us an opportunity to revisit our potentially dark past. Which the ego holds on to tightly, because it wants to be right or to win at any cost.

As we move forward in opening the heart, thoughts of the past will always arise. Maybe even more than we would like to have them occur. However, it is our choice then to be aware of these thoughts and not embrace passing negativity when it arises.

We can offer up gratitude for the passing thoughts and simply release them and let them go, as they have served to show or teach us some lessons. Moving forward they offer us no value other than some awareness.

How can we start on a road of personal forgiveness? Simply by not passing judgment! One of our purposes in life is to not make any judgments of others and, most importantly, not of ourselves. Forgiveness gives us back the power to perform a healing process on and for ourselves.

Once this is embraced, we now will have the ability to offer these seeds of forgiveness, growth and healing to others.

If it is truly your desire to open your heart, then it is up to you to live up to this affirmation or conviction, and you yourself must make every effort to bring about this change. The Bible says to "love one another, as you in turn love yourself." The Bible doesn't place any restriction or limit to who will be the beneficiaries of this open heart, this love we offer. By giving love we will touch others, who will in turn do the same. Although, keep in mind that an intended recipient chooses whether to receive the offer of love—and that choice doesn't require our involvement.

When we unconditionally give love to others, we will never know what impact this could have on our world. Our personal world encompasses as much or as little as we choose to expand. So why not give of yourself and give without attachment? Who are we to place expectations on our love? Expectations are never a benefit; applying them is, however, an act of selfishness or possibly even some self-serving motive.

• • •

Now, let's look at the receivers of our love. If they don't give this gift of love to others, it is not up to us to pass judgment, we have done our best and that is truly enough. We have no control over others, and we need to be mindful of our own actions. All we can control is ourselves, and that is enough and in some cases a challenge!

Sometimes the hardest person to offer love to, is ourself. Why? Because we know all of our own pasts, close up and personal. To heal others by the act of forgiveness, we must first accept forgiveness for ourselves and our own past actions.

As I have said before in speeches and presentations: if the horse is dead, get off it! Carrying around un-forgiven acts of the past is truly a burden that no one should endure. Carrying this burden can be self-inflicting pain.

Furthermore there is no future in being your own personal martyr. If anyone really feels a calling to be a martyr, think for a moment, do others really care? Probably not! Do you really think other people have nothing better to do with their lives than to support your personal martyrdom? Where is the love? Can a pity party supply lasting love? I think not.

Forgiveness is transforming, not only for us personally, but it also impacts the lives of others and can then spread out to our communities.

How could that be possible? By the change in our attitudes/perspectives, we will view our issues or even our world differently. And perhaps so will those we come in contact with. There is a domino effect.

This journey of forgiveness is not for the weak of heart. As we all know, it is always easy to fall back into past experiences, reactions or past dramas. It is for the strongly committed person, who wants to live in and from a better place. Being aware allows us to make better choices. Think how calm your demeanor will be when you offer forgiveness unconditionally. In other words, unconditional love, which results from the opening of one's heart.

Will this process take time? Remember that there is no time except for this moment right now; the past is past, the future has not yet arrived. This so-called timing could be entirely based on our personal ability to forgive ourselves. As with so many other things, we have learned by our awareness, this could take a long time or it could happen in an instant. It all depends on us and our resistance or reluctance to forgive and offer love.

Many things can lead us to un-forgiveness: injustice, deep hurt, conflicts, lies, and the list could go on and on. What is the real point of justifying an act of un-forgiveness? There is none, whatsoever. But these few examples above came from outside oneself and then have been embraced and/or internalized as one's own.

Why then would anyone choose to stay stuck in a state of un-forgiveness—perhaps because of the drama it invites or incites internally? That's my perception, and I don't see any reason to remain in an unhealthy state of un-forgiveness whatsoever. Do I fall back and stumble? Well I am human? Then the answer is obvious.

Let's take a look at some potential health aspects of acting with an open heart versus an un-opened heart. The open heart is totally un-encumbered and free from *dis-ease*. With open-heartedness, you are in a state of calmness and peacefulness. So you could say "I'm good!" If our hearts and therefore our bodies are at ease there can be no "dis."

One way that we allow this lack of ease to happen within ourselves is though stress. The medical community has periodically stated that stress is a silent killer. It robs us of life-supporting energy, which we all need. It can close down functions that the body normally performs with ease and can produce mental anguish along with a host of other symptoms. (Please keep in mind that I am not a doctor and these are personal feeling and thoughts.)

How could or does this happen? Maybe because somewhere along the way, we have accepted an illusion as a truth. So we can be looking at both aspects, mental and physical dis-ease.

When will we learn the lessons offered to us by many wise mystics, gurus and most importantly Jesus? Sorry to say, but it is often when we each find ourselves boxed into a corner by our own personal issues or tragedies. And feel that we don't have any alterative!

This is when the feeling of not having any choice washes over us, and we feel lost or without hope. For those of us that reach this point and make a different positive choice, we very possibility could have saved our own lives. This last sentence comes from my own personal experiences.

Circumstances such as these usually require life changes. Some may be easy, others may offer more challenges. Whatever the case, it requires some personal choices. And we can be grateful for this awareness, thus being able to re-choose.

When confronted with choices, choose honestly from the heart. Open your heart and let go of the dreaded stuff, which is clogging you or slowing you down. What is the purpose of "stuff" anyway? Only I know about my personal road blocks—this stuff. You on the other hand would only know about your personal road blocks—your stuff. When a state of awareness occurs within you, then and only then, can you make a choice or a better choice.

So when should you start, this opening of your heart process? How about now! Open your heart and let the light of God's love, higher power, spirit, spiritual guides, angels, the universe, whatever is your choice of words, into your heart. It is within this light, this warm glow, where your true potential lies, and only you have the key and can stake your claim to a new and different life. Again, remember you are the maker of your own choices, so open your heart and choose wisely.

Personal notes...

*P*ersonal notes...

The Art of Listening

You may say *what* does "the art of listening" mean? It can seem very simple, like NOT TALKING, although there is really a lot more involved. You must be consciously connected and aware of where the speaker is, as well as what they need or are wanting at that moment from you, the listener. This is a challenge for a lot of people. Think about the above statement for a moment—how many people do you know who can truly just listen?

Do you realize what an incredible gift you are giving another person, by your ability to quietly listen? We can then begin to feel a sense of peacefulness wash over our being. To be a listener takes practice, because most people want to enter into and be part of the dialog. Sometimes the person doing the talking just would like a compassionate listener.

How could we become a *compassionate* listener? Some people may view being a compassionate listener incorrectly—they think it requires doing something, giving some response and being verbally involved. Please understand that's not true. By listening, you are or can be very involved. In fact you may be filling a void the speaker has in themselves. And all you have to do is be a good listener.

That is, you have to stay connected to what the other person is saying and feeling. You must be present, in this very moment. And give the other person your undivided attention. Then you'll be able to sense a person's feeling by their words, tone and inflection. Don't allow yourself to drift off, paying attention to your own thoughts running around in your head. A person will sense your lack of interest and might very likely close down. And that could be at the very moment when your listening ability could or would be most appreciated and be of its greatest value to the speaker!

This person needs and deserves your undivided attention, particularly when they trust you enough to tell you about something personal within their lives. Remember the Lord gave us two ears and one mouth. It would be to our benefit to use them wisely.

Here are a couple other expressions I've heard over time: "A closed mouth gathers no feet," and "Sometimes a person will open their mouth just to change feet." Have you even felt that you could personally relate to these expressions? If your answer is "No," are you really being honest! Okay, I believe you—I think?

I've talked about this gift you are giving the person speaking by your ability to listen, yet the gift is also received by you. Because the speaker also gives you the gift of *allowing you to listen* to their innermost thoughts, troubles, pain or perhaps even happiness, what they are really needing most from you is validation of their worth at a potentially low point in life. Hence you are giving them this wonderful gift by giving your full attention and letting there be no doubt that you are hearing every word and its full meaning. To do otherwise turns the attention to you and takes it away from their feelings and their potentially needed validation.

Remember, they have just given you a glimpse of their heart and soul. You cannot solve their problem or concerns, although by allowing them to verbalize whatever is troubling them without judging, they can then move forward to better work out the issue for themselves.

Perhaps it comes down to this: when someone tells you something, it's not that you need to know it, but rather that they need to tell you something troubling their heart, their being. Please remember to offer, and give, the precious gift of listening.

In so many cases, the person doing the listening can't stand not being involved verbally, because they have started to form their own answers to resolve the speaker's issues or situations. If the person doing the speaking wants your comments, they most certainly will ask you for your input. So remember, "a closed mouth gathers *no* feet."

How many times have you been listening to a person and felt you had an answer, and then you did it—you interrupted? This very likely could have been at a point in the conversation where the speaker most wanted your listening abilities.

In fact, the person speaking wasn't looking for answers or comments anyway, certainly not then. They just wanted to be heard. Keeping silent instead gives the person speaking another level of confidence in your commitment to be a good listener for them.

To extend the concept of listening: Do you know the difference between praying and meditating? Well, whenever we are in any form of praying, we are talking to God, a higher power, or whatever term you choose to use. In prayer sometimes we are asking for something, or being grateful for something that has happened in our lives. (If a person is going toward blame, that is a whole other subject, which I will not address at this time.)

This is definitely a one-way conversation, and you are doing the speaking. To carry this thought a little further, it's with our faith knowing that God is listening.

Now, when we embark upon meditation, things are different. First we might have to work a bit to quiet our busy minds; this can be a challenge in the beginning. And it usually requires practice, practice, and more practice.

Once this state of mind is attained, we can start to hear on an entirely new and different level. It is amazing! We will have an opportunity to hear what God has for us. Some might want to call it: what the Universe has for us. Notice I didn't say that God would answer our prayers and questions. Because what is being offered to us is more valuable and is something we need, at a deeper level. So listen!

A lot of people want what they want, and don't want to allow for something different, like what the Lord may be offering. It's not about what you want; it's about you being able to accept what is being offered you, and it could be something you truly need! So it might just be worth our listening.

Now, let's say we can agree that listening has some real power and value. Then it is within the silence of listening that our answers can be revealed on this journey we call life. Not only is that true for ourselves, it is also true for others on their own personal journeys.

When we allow a person to express themselves and we listen intently, we have offered them another wonderful gift, that of our calmness, which the other person can sense by our quiet demeanor. Holding a calm quiet place for another gives that person permission to enter and explore this place of calming energy for themselves.

Once within a state of calmness, the speaker will have opportunities to open up and reveal what they are truly needing or feeling. Within this state of peacefulness, a person can find relief to some of life's situations.

Such an opportunity allows for revealing of answers to be heard, seen and felt by any person in need.

Here is another point, which is the art of *learning to listen*. When we just listen we are then freed as well as relieved of any obligation in giving advice to another, either wanted or unwanted. Now when we move from being "listener" to contributing, we have engaged ourselves into a conversation, perhaps into somewhere we should not be involved.

The dynamics have changed—as a listener, you may have been respected. By opening your mouth and speaking you became verbally involved. What could even be worse is that now you could be viewed as taking sides! Wow, and this all happened by the opening of a mouth.

Okay, so isn't it calming to just be the listener? Furthermore, when the listener's mouth opened at an inappropriate time, the one with the big mouth, who should have been listening, might now be viewed as anything but wise.

This reminds me of a story. At a party was this person who didn't say anything, or very little, only listened intently and nodded politely.

Some of the other people started to say how wise this person was.

Conversely, there was another person who wanted to be noticed, and made sure everyone knew who he or she was by giving suggestions, advice or comments. Well, that person was surely noticed and thought of poorly, as generally foolish.

Which brings me to yet another saying: "A person can be viewed as wise by not speaking—or they can open their mouth and remove all doubt as to whether they are wise or a fool." Now how would you want people to think of you? If you speak, speak only a little and speak very carefully. And enjoy the wisdom of your wise quietness.

Until you understand what it is to be a good listener you may have no idea of its true value or potential. Do you even realize who receives the value when you offer yourself as a listener?

Believe me, a lot of what is received or gained isn't just for the speaker alone. You, the listener, will receive a huge benefit as well. This could increase your own sense of value and well being, along with bringing your life some additional balance.

There are certainly times when we allow ourselves to get into our own way, so it's important to remember we are all passengers on this journey, and certainly not doing the driving. When we listen, we afford ourselves an opportunity to learn.

How many times have you been able to learn something when your mouth was in motion? Generally not many! In some cases, the mouth is or was on fast-forward. Remember when our mouth is in motion, our ears are generally closed!

As I sit here on my deck and listen, I can hear the creaking of the neighbors' swing a couple of houses down from me. When was the last time you allowed yourself the time to just sit and hear the wind gently blowing through the trees or heard someone else's wind chimes?

Be gentle to yourself and start to appreciate all that can be appreciated. This is a form of the same process that allows you to transpose yourself into a person that can truly "just listening."

It all starts when we work at listening and putting our random thoughts behind us, for one small moment, then the next moment, and the next and the next.

All of a sudden we are a tuned to our surroundings and all they have or could offer. This is a moment-by-moment experience that you receive by listening. Thank you for just listening!

Personal notes...

Personal notes...

Coming from Love

When you read the title of this chapter, "Coming from Love," what thoughts did it provoke in your mind? Or, instead perhaps it was a feeling, which could have come from your heart. What do you think started this stirring within?

All that you sense, feel or think have come about because of your increased ability to be aware. This allows for a refreshing new aspect of our lives. And it continually develops as we also develop in our own process of personal growth. Isn't it wonderful that now we can be aware not only of our own thoughts but we can also tune in to the feelings we are experiencing?

We could be truly acting in the role of the observer of our own universe. In love there is no passage of judgment, nothing needs be done other than offer love and observe. However we decide to choose, it is of our choosing.

How best would it be to describe this subject? The absolute best place for me to get a true and honest description would be to consult the Bible. Although there are many passages on love in the Bible, this is the one I have chosen, because it seems to speak to me and has for a long time. This answer below offers us both, what love is as well as what it is not.

> *Love is patient, love is kind. It does not envy, it does not boast, it is not proud. It is not rude, it is not self-seeking, it is not easily angered and it keeps no record of wrongs. Love does not delight in evil but rejoices with the truth. It always protects, always trusts, always hopes and always preserves. Love never fails…*
>
> 1st Corinthians 13: 4–8

So what is "coming from LOVE?" It really is those above attributes. Basically it's our personal attitude toward life, this life that we share with others or interface with on a regular basis. Love is unencumbered, has nothing it's carrying around as baggage, and is free.

When a person thinks of love, it can bring to the mind's eye something peaceful and gentle. A place that is within and untouched by the turmoil of the busyness of our daily life.

How wonderful when we feel we are in love with and loved by another person! It is enhanced even more when we realize we have this love for ourselves—it is our true foundation. It can seem that the entire world revolves around that other person, when you're in love with someone and the relationship is new.

However, this could be an ego trap. Why, you may ask? Because perhaps you may have set some expectations for this or from this loved one. And when those expectations are not fulfilled it produces an entire range of different emotions that could lead to stress. Which, in reality, is a state of unbalance within our own preserved perspective.

In this state of unrest none of the potential outcomes are really true, because they have been developed within our own minds and perhaps the ego has interceded. The easiest way to avoid such an event is to not to have any attachments or any expectations. And always a good way to resolve such situations would be through honest communications and forgiveness.

• • •

If you want to "come from love," always keep your heart open and your communications honest and clear. As, say, opposed to saying something vague or having some type of agenda, as in the manner of manipulation.

I read, not so long ago, that an important aspect of this journey in our personal development is not the great strides we may make with one another, although they are important as well.

When the day is done and we sit in quiet retrospect, have we become a better person today than we were yesterday, or even a better person from one moment to the next moment? If this is the case, then your love energy has increased not only for yourself; because it, this energy, will flow out and enhance the lives of others you touch, either seen or unseen.

Growth can't be expected without some challenges along the way. These challenges will come to us in the form of lessons. How we view these lessons is up to us, whether with dread, in trepidation and fear, or open to a blessing yet to be unveiled.

During challenging times, it can be difficult to see the lesson—or any lesson for that matter. Let alone embrace these lessons with a sense of gratefulness and gratitude! This is where the ability to quiet the mind and go within to seek the answers comes into play. For the answers are truly all within us. And these answers will be shown to us at exactly the proper time, when they will serve our highest good and perhaps even add value to our lives.

Can this growth be expected without our personal involvement in learning? Not likely! When a situation presents itself, it is our ability to investigate and our desire for a better life in the future that offer the seeds that motivate us forward.

How do we get to this point of understanding? By the failures of the past—or perhaps better wording would be to say, the lessons we learned through those experiences. If we produce a better life for ourselves by the choices we have made, we can then offer a higher level of energy to humanity in general. We are not in or of this world as individuals alone, we are each part of humanity as a whole.

I would choose to define passion in the following manner. Passion is our ability to harness the power of good within us and to move us to the next higher level of consciousness in our lives. It is not done by looking at a situation with the same eyes we have used in the past and expecting different results. It may only come by our choosing to view a situation from a different perspective. Passion excites our essence; it kindles the fires within our bodies, minds and spirits.

There is a difference between power and force. This is a power of unlimited energy. Power flows naturally with the energy of the universe, whereas force is unnatural to the flow of energy. Like when something is forced upon us and does not feel good to our very core.

Where are the challenges when coming from love? They certainly are not from an environment of our own relationships, or are they? Like the relationships we have with family and friends. At times, these challenges are well hidden within the veil of various mystics, current deceptions or past ones. When these challenges arise, could they be the ego's diversions from a loving heart, to its playground of negativity?

At times such as these, we might even buy into an unloving experience, which may have started in our own minds and then worked its way out in our actions. Or maybe it is what we have chosen as our perception.

At times this perception is self-induced because of past experiences. If it's negative, don't bring it forward into the present and then proceed on into the future. Anything that we sense ourselves is entirely our own personal perception, which could be illusory.

When a situation arises with another person, perhaps that person is calling for love at some deeper level than their current awareness/consciousness. Remembering this allows for a more peaceful solution. Let me examine the word "remember," looking at it as connecting or reconnecting with another, thus "*re*-membering," to join or rejoin.

We are all one, all joined together at a higher spiritual level.

The answer in a negative situation can be found in something as simple as remaining calm, peaceful and quiet; this very act might offer the other person the ability to accept your calming energy.

When we or another person is in a state of agitation, it may be difficult to be aware of this calming energy. So then perhaps all we should remember is that, once we're re-connected to our higher level of awareness, we must give love, pure and simple.

By not engaging in any confrontation, we allow ourselves to act as observer, without judgment, without attachment. By giving love we allow this energy of peacefulness to emanate from our core being, giving freely, without expectations, to those in need. Then we can possibly start planting the seeds of personal growth within our minds and subsequently our hearts.

So, what type of plants shall we grow and nourish in the gardens of our minds? As in most gardens, there are weeds. How do our mental weeds start to grow? Basically, they begin by the lack of attention to what we allow in as thoughts.

Therefore we must be on a constant vigil of the thoughts coming into our minds. If we tend to grow nourishing and loving thoughts, we will produce the blooms of loving energy. We are the masters of our thoughts, thus our energy, so which would you chose for yourself and give out to this universe? What could be our greatest guiding presence in this realm of the universe, in a single word, I would call it "love."

If we consider that we are here on this earth as loving spiritual beings, then it could be said we are spiritual beings having a human experience. In our past thinking we may have occasionally experienced some spiritual events from time to time. When in actuality the converse could more than likely be true.

Another way to consider this is that God (or higher power) is interwoven into the fabric of our lives. Centuries ago, during some battle, a soldier said to his general, "Isn't it a blessing that God is on our side?" To which the general answered, "I would much prefer having the blessing that we are on God's side!"

In reality, then, who is the leader and who are the followers? The answer is intuitively obvious. We could then go a bit further with saying that the Holy Spirit will never enter a person where the Holy Spirit is uninvited. Now we have additional seeds of responsibility.

It is our responsibility to do our part and acknowledge where we are and where we would like to go with our lives. If we look at life as a "mode of transportation," we then need to get on board. That too is our choice.

Let's look, for a moment, at the opposite to coming from love. What does this look like, withholding love from someone? What have we really done? Consider that we are pure energy and now we have restricted this energy flow. Who does it hurt? First of all, it would be the person doing the withholding, ourselves, more than everyone else involved.

Now this fear or negativity has been put in motion. Lives could be hurt or changed by this negative energy or the lack of loving energy. And it can be felt far beyond the realm of our personal realization.

How does something like this happen? I think it could possibly start with unresolved self-love issues. At least these are issues that people carry around within their minds. You see, we must love ourselves first before we can truly come from love. It you don't have love within yourself, you certainly can't offer love to others.

Where is our largest opportunity to practice "Coming from Love"? How about the area of family dynamics? This can be the single most-challenging source of experiences. Because of their nature things from this source can occur over and over again.

Why do you think these happen with more regularity? Because we could have past life-experiences with these individuals and know their hot buttons. As we recognize these hot buttons in others, it is important to also remember that we have these hot buttons ourselves.

We can't see something unless we also recognize the same thing as part of our fiber. That's what realization is, it's our ability to see, and be aware. Then where is the blessing? It sure isn't in the act of engagement. Engagement might only continue the issues or conflicts. Why would we get caught or allow ourselves to be drawn into something like this?

Another question would be, Where is the value, or even better yet the redeeming value? Sometimes just acknowledging a situation is enough. What do we desire of any situation? Peace! Our job, once we notice that we're "off our peace," is to make a choice and return to peacefulness for our higher good as well as for those around us.

When we find ourselves off our peace, we must become aware; once awareness occurs we can then make better choices to return to love. Is this easy? I would say that, at first, it's absolutely not! However, we can and will improve, by the simple desire for this state of peacefulness, and our openness to the opportunities to be patient and then practice, practice, practice.

So when someone in our lives offers up a situation that has drawn them off their peace, we may want to view it as a calling for love. When you are the observer you now can see clearer and offer more love. Holding love in your heart for the other, and offering love's energy to another human, is a huge gift to that individual.

In family dynamics, when a situation or a set of issues arises, what happens most of the time? When we get sucked into a situation, now remember we alone allowed that to happen. And you alone made that choice, so don't go blaming another person.

Again, awareness is a foundation. Did you really want to engage in this situation? The answer is obvious, but now that we're in the situation, we can elect to re-choose. So don't be foolish enough to make a stand, particularly if it is something that is uncomfortable. Make the change, and re-choose peacefulness.

Sometimes the question is: Do we want to be right or do we want to be peaceful? How could we have handled this confrontational situation differently? Don't engage, but offer unconditional love in such situations. When we choose not to engage, perhaps we are offering acceptance to their issues or the situation. A better venue for our involvement could be in our ability to just listen (meaning, saying nothing).

There are certainly times when a person in distress isn't asking you for a resolution; they might be merely asking to be heard. Listening is just listening, not forming answers and not talking. For most people this is a real challenge.

I would like to tell you a true story that is unfolding as I am writing this chapter. And I am only an observer. It involves three people: Jim, a person off his peace; Gail, a person not wanting to engage and aggravate things further; and then we have Bill, the object of the brewing situation. (Of course the names have been changed for obvious reasons.)

All are highly skilled, trained professionals. Jim and Gail are opposed in their views of the situation as well as the outcome, which is directed toward Bill. Hence we have a drama unfolding.

Jim, who happens to be coming from a position of power, holds most of the cards. I use the word "power" loosely, although in this case it is more in the realm of force. Because Jim will not allow any room for negotiations other than what is acceptable in his view. If things don't go to his liking, he can enforce his will and his decisions, no matter what.

From the observer's viewpoint we might be able to see some things differently, although by his actions he seems to be aggressively negative towards Bill. In truth, he might have some deeper issues to resolve within himself. Because of what I observe, I think he has made a choice and will not allow his view to be fogged by logic or compassion. He is an example of being stuck in his choice. I can also see that he's uncomfortable, and will not change his mind because he won't allow himself to lose face. How would you like to have that internal turmoil?

The sad thing, in my perception, is that he is completely unaware. So how can he make a different choice? He's right and he's right, in his own mind. I also think, because of what I have observed, that there is some fear involved, yet he might be unaware of this fact as well.

When a person is being negatively aggressive toward another, it isn't about the person that the hostility is directed towards; it's about the person directing the turmoil. So when a situation arises, remember if you are having this reaction, then it is about some unresolved issues within yourself.

Now let's move on to Gail. She is not at the same level within the organization as Jim. Hence, she doesn't hold any of the cards; however, what she holds is logic and compassion. Can her voice, her opinion, be heard? she has asked, and answered, "sadly no."

When she has attempted to offer some suggestions, she has been told not to push the issues, which will only make the situation more difficult for Bill. She is attempting to bring a different perspective or different view of the situation in an attempt to look for a more peaceful resolution.

I would like to look at the difference levels of life giving energy. In his book, *Power vs. Force,* David Hawkins talks about the energy or power that is within each person and the different corresponding levels of energy. When we look at a person such as Mother Teresa, we see a high level of life-giving energy and intuitive consciousness. Then at the other end of the spectrum we have what could be called force. In this book, it is termed as lower levels of energy.

An example of this lower level of energy could be found within a person such as a political dictator (which is not a reference to Jim). The determinable differences reside in their energy levels and levels of consciousness, or perhaps in the lack thereof.

You may ask, what about Bill? Well, he is aware of the dynamics of the different personalities and the situation in general. I had an opportunity to talk, or more specifically, to listen to Bill.

This is what I heard: He knows the situation is unfolding and it may not be to his liking, and he has chosen not to become part of this drama and remain at a level of calmness. I asked him, what will you do? I thought his answer was insightful. He said, "I will hold love for Jim and will not move from this point of love."

As was said by Jesus, "for he knows not what he is doing." Where is the joy of wanting to enter into negative energy, when there can be love? What good is served by restricting love's energy? None. Thus, Bill said "I will not enter into judgment, or unloving thoughts. I am in control of my own thoughts and my own personal state of peacefulness."

What an incredible view that I was lucky enough to witness! To me it shows unrestricted love for humanity. Thank you, Bill, for your love and kindness; you offer a light unto the world. You have left a fingerprint on my heart that I will not forget easily. And now I have also shared your story with others.

Would you like to feel more love and joy in your life? Then do life's ordinary tasks with extraordinary love. For there are no boundaries when we are receiving the love of God.

So why would we build walls and make limitations within and for ourselves? It has also been said that only thoughts of love are true thoughts; all the rest are the illusions we paint in our lives. What everlasting elements do we really have in this world?—it's either love, which is truth, or non-love, which is un-truths.

Perhaps another way to move towards this goal is to think only loving thoughts. When this occurs, miracles will start to happen in your life and in the lives you touch. So be aware of all the goodness coming your way and be grateful. Remember this process starts within you. Will you be an instrument of positive energy (love) or negative energy? Which would you choose?

When we have an opportunity to view or experience bad things happening in our lives or others' lives, we could be tempted to adapt thoughts of blame and then to blame God.

A truth about God's love is not that he has allowed bad things to happen to good people. His promise is that He will always be there, with us through those difficult times, with His unconditional everlasting love.

Think for a moment. If our actions are truly felt by the universe, what would we want to leave behind on or in the universe? There is a theory called the butterfly effect. That theory states that if a butterfly flaps its wings in Asia, the results are felt in North America.

Now let's say we can accept and agree

with this theory. Then what effect would our thoughts have on the universe? It could be un-believable good—that's if our thoughts are for the higher good of all in this universe.

As with the butterfly in Asia, it may never know the effect it has started, although it has been felt both there and here. So please consider this: each of us can have a profound effect on this earth by expressing thoughts and acts of love to other humans.

Each of us, with the simplest thought, act or feeling of love, has the potential to gener-ate more love, person to person, one moment at a time, moment to moment. Why would we choose anything else! Come from love and leave nothing but love behind as your legacy.

P.S. "The rest of the story": As was expected, Bill's outcome was not good, and he got rail-roaded. That comment came from Gail and was her impression. Was the outcome right, fair or just? I'll leave that as a thought to be pondered or just let go. From my perception the only per-son that was satisfied with the outcome was the person who was also oblivious.

Personal notes...

Personal notes...

Forgiveness

What is forgiveness? For me it is a state of *being,* and or a state of mind.

When I am forgiving I am more at peace with the world and all that is within this world. Conversely, when I am unforgiving I can be in a state of unrest, uncomfortable, moody or even agitated. Not a good place to be mentally or emotionally.

And how did I get to such a negative point? It could have been by the act of not forgiving someone or something. It's up to me as well as the resulting perception I am holding onto in the first place. So, what's it to be—forgiveness or not allowing forgiveness? Because it could all start with me or you. Now if you're thinking that not allowing forgiveness gives you some power, your ego just kicked in.

How do we get to forgiveness? What does it take to forgive? It's quite simple really; all you need to do is say "I forgive you" and mean it. When you say "I forgive you," that is your opportunity to let this issue go, not to be brought up again. Because when it is brought up again or thrown back is a person's face; it was not really an act of true forgiveness. Remember: it's past, it's done, let it go, let it be, and forgive.

That's only the start and there's more to this act of forgiveness. The joy and the peacefulness you'll experience can be unbounded. It's amazing how those words "I forgive you" have changed the lives of so many people. Certainly, they have changed the life of the person expressing forgiveness, because in their heart they have truly forgiven the other person. For the person receiving those words, it allows them also to move on with their life, if they so choose.

Forgiveness is such a loving gentle thing to do. If we are honestly forgiving, it has great value. However it you are casually stating a formula and are going to bring the issue up later, that isn't forgiveness—not even close.

Casual forgiveness could be a way of attempting to manipulate another person to get what you want. Forgiveness should be without attachments or expectations. If you are only casually forgiving then you are forgiving with some personal agenda in mind. Forgiveness is about letting go of the situation, so that you may start rebuilding within your own life.

Perhaps one of the biggest questions that may come up is that the person wants to know, "Why should I forgive someone who has maybe wronged me?" An example: Why should I forgive another person, it wasn't my fault, it was something they did or said to me or about me.

The reason you forgive is to allow yourself the possibility to move on—as in, on with your life. Furthermore, there is no reason to carry any baggage of *un-forgiveness* any longer.

If you look back and ask yourself "What good did this un-forgiveness serve?," you'll probably come up with an answer like "It really only served my ego. And it only served to keep me stuck or to keep me from finding peace for myself. It did not allow me to move back to the peacefulness that I would like to have, and deserve in my life." This is an important realization or awareness.

Allow me to share a little secret with you

on forgiveness. One of the ways in which forgiveness can have a real impact is to make it personally important to you. Once this is done it could have a greater impact on the person you are forgiving or asking forgiveness from.

When you are talking to someone about forgiveness, either asking for or expressing forgiveness, it is extremely important to be truthful and honest, and express your feelings in a loving manner.

Then what you are saying will have a better chance of being perceived the way in which you had intended. One of the ways to strengthen your message and have greater success that your thoughts are being received the way you would like, is to silently say to yourself "I love you" then ask for forgiveness or give your forgiveness.

This would also work for forgiveness of yourself, by simply saying "I love you" and "please forgive me" or even saying "I forgive you." These words can have enormous benefits.

It isn't necessary to get into all the details surrounding the situation, and they really aren't important at this particular time. Because it's more likely those involved have been through the details before and there are no reasons to

bring up unnecessary pain. With this act of forgiveness, it allows for time to start the healing
process for those involved, and it's time to let go
of the issues because it really is in the past.

Keep in mind that you would like the other
person on a similar wavelength, so that she or
he isn't caught off guard. If that happens, then
by all means let them know what is on your
mind and where you're coming from.

Remember that whatever is fresh in your
mind may not be in the other person's. Therefore if it is your desire to be understood, it is
up to you to take advantage of communicating
with them properly. Both to be understood as to
where you are coming from, and why you are in
this particular state of mind at the moment.

The main idea here is to accomplish your
resolution and to start the healing for both or all
parties involved. Then you might be able to feel
the ensuing peace of mind and spirit that will
more than likely follow.

Always attempt to speak in plain and simple language so that the communications are understood completely. Be honest, truthful, loving
and compassionate with your choice of words.
The results of this can possibly change your life
and those involved. That's what this discussion

is really about, finding peace or closure, because this is for all those involved. Not just one person. Will others also find peace and resolution? They will have the same opportunity—what they do with it is up to them, not you.

To have this work effectively, both parties should be in a peaceful place, emotionally and mentally ready to give and receive what is being offered. If either person is too busy to concentrate, hold off for a more favorable time and setting.

Be patient—it's worth the time and effort, it's for the peacefulness of our bodies, minds and spirits. Both people should be actively present in that particular moment, to understand what is being expressed. Because the words "I forgive you" should be expressed from the person's heart. Love is always being forgiving.

Perhaps one of the people involved isn't even aware that they can achieve peacefulness through forgiveness. Maybe the person has only had a brief encounter with peacefulness and it has lasted for the shortest of time. They might even wonder if they were dreaming. Then they are quickly engulfed in their old patterns of busyness and perhaps even turmoil. This turmoil could be from other unresolved issues troubling that person, so that they feel no relief from any-thing or anyone.

What a sad position to be in, in life. Life shouldn't and doesn't have to be lived with the feeling of being overwhelmed with troubles or various burdens.

When we hold un-forgiveness in our minds and hearts we are essentially building up walls between ourselves and other people.

Do you think you can speak to another person through the wall that you have constructed so soundly and that you even have an opportunity of being heard? Keep in mind it's always diffi-cult having any communication heard through thick walls. What is the reason for building such a fortress of un-forgiveness?

It only tends to restrict and hold or keep a person bound and it's all within the individual. It can be a challenging task to forgive and tear down those walls, and yet it must be done.

Here are a couple of personal stories as ex-amples.

Some time after my second divorce, my ex-wife and I were both at the same event. We were talking and all of a sudden she said, "I for-give you." It caught me off guard as I didn't expect anything like that. Although, it seemed strange at the time that she would even say "I forgive you." I just listened and let it go.

Yet I thought about the comment a lot, as well as its implications. You may ask, Did you know what she was talking about? Absolutely! I have to admit it did take me some period of time to really understand what she was saying and meaning. Now, thinking back, I am grateful.

This act allowed her closure for herself, as she was letting go. And now it was up to me to do the same and find peace and closure for myself. When I understood the impact of "I forgive you" between us, I could then lovingly embrace and accept the closure for myself.

The next incident happened between my niece and me, and I won't go into all the details. We were having a phone conversation about her physical health. And I commented, "Don't you think you should accept some of the responsibility for you own personal health?" Her response was other than favorable, and I was told not to call her again.

We do see each other from time to time at various family gatherings. I have made it a point to talk to her. Although it is apparent that my forgiveness from her is not forthcoming. So I now feel the best way to resolve this situation, which is also the simplest, would be for me to honestly ask for her forgiveness, the next time we are together.

When you forgive others, it makes it easier for others to forgive you. True forgiveness is a state of heart. Forgiveness is like a two-sided coin; one side is the forgiveness that you offer to others, the other side is the forgiveness that you ask from others for yourself. True forgiveness isn't somewhere "out there." It starts within ourselves individually.

And forgiveness is not a one-time activity or event, it's not like you can forgive someone and you're done. Because forgiveness is forever, and you should work at constantly being is a state of forgiveness to all. That will allow forgiveness to come back to you, because you have freely given forgiveness to others.

Personal notes...

Personal notes...

Someone Hurt My Feelings

What would prompt a person to make such a statement as this chapter's title? When I hear it I want to just shake the person. Then I allow myself to return to a calmer state and say to that person, "Do you realize that no one can hurt your feelings? Or does the person making this remark realize how untrue this statement really is? Keep in mind we are talking about feelings here."

Only you (the receiver of comments) have the power to make that leap of faith within your mind. What's sad is if the receiver of hurtful comments believes them. When we realize that we all have our own personal power regarding our feelings, why would anyone choose to give this power to someone else? Or, accept the belief that someone other than ourselves has any power over our own feelings?

Once you realize that you are in complete control of your own personal feelings, your life can become calmer. Then we can begin to understand that no one can ever hurt our feelings. Only we ourselves can attach some meaning or perception to another person's words, issues or situations—as well as to any comments directed towards ourselves.

Why would a person allow someone else the control to take our personal beliefs? It could be because he or she is looking for something outside themselves. Or someone to save them, take care of them, or perhaps even love them. This could happen from either lack or need. Neither is a good sign, and it could be a sign of some imbalance within their lives.

When a situation arises and you realize that someone has said something hurtful towards you or anyone else, what should you do? It's important to realize that the comments are really about the person talking or making the accusations. There is some comfort in this understanding, because then you recognize this person may be coming from deeper issues within themselves. Something has happened within that person's life that they have accepted, either consciously or unconsciously, and it's affecting their disposition and personality at that time. They could be striking out at anyone—in this case you have been the chosen target!

You may have noticed a similarity between the person supplying the hurtful comments and the receiving person. That's because the resulting actions are feeding on one another, and can be essentially the same issues viewed from different sides.

How can this be? Perhaps they are both needy or both instinctively relate to the other's request for love or neediness. Also the roles could change at any moment. So if you are that person receiving some hurtful comments, just listen and realize that it's "not about you." Don't engage, because that is what the other person is attempting to accomplish. They may want to draw you into their drama.

Also, we as humans are generally either coming from love (thus offering love) or asking for love (looking for love), to come into our lives. When this is realized we can become more compassionate and understanding towards all humanity.

Sometimes a person's request for love is

wrapped in different forms; it could be anger, re-sentment, hatred, bitterness, jealousy or a host of other negativities. (Which, by the way, may be an effect of the ego.) When someone is asking for love, listen to what is being said—not only to the words, but also the meaning between or behind the words.

A person can be wanting to draw attention to themselves. Think about it: when a baby cries, it is looking for attention. Yes, it could be to get a diaper changed. Babies generally cry for one of three reasons: food ("Hey, Mom, it's my feed-ing time"), warmth (needing clothes or a warm blanket) or wetness (needing to be changed). Yet the most important reason is because the in-fant wants to be loved, held and generally feel wanted. But hey—a lot of adults feel the same way.

Children do a remarkable job of searching out different ways to draw attention to them-selves and away from someone or something else. And these patterns can be carried on into adult life.

Then if problems arise, a person without aware-ness may think they do not have the ability to re-choose for themselves. Most of us have seen situations like this in action, and can admit that we are or can now be more aware. Make no mistake, feeling hurt is reaching out for something, and we can call that something "LOVE."

It is within our ability to embrace this fact, and then we can become peaceful observers of the various storms that enter our lives. Thus, we will be able to offer love in whatever form seems fitting to a situation at a particular time.

You may be wondering what all this has to do with a person's feelings. Keep in mind that feelings are full of different emotions, and they can have an effect on a person's statements as well as their moods.

How can we resolve some of these feelings? Maybe just by listening. With your heart open and without any attachments or judgments, you may be of assistance. So, by holding a loving place of calmness and peace for another, we have offered them peacefulness for themselves. Which will in turn come back to us—what goes around comes around.

Years ago I read a book called *The Four Agreements* by Don Miguel Ruiz.

His four agreements are:
1. Be Impeccable with Your Word.
2. Don't Take Anything Personally.
3. Don't Make Assumptions.
4. Always Do Your Best.

These may seem easy enough to understand, although they can present a challenge to live by from time to time. Here again, these are good things to be aware of on our journey through life. It is our choice to offer love and compassion. So why would we withhold? Remember, "Don't Take Anything Personally." That way you won't *get* your feelings hurt.

Personal notes...

Personal notes...

Non-Attachment or Attachment

Allow me to start this subject by first looking at the meaning of the word attachment. It's described in the dictionary as a feeling that binds one to a person, thing, cause, idea or the like; a profound attachment to something or someone. Here we'll also be discussing "non-attachment," which will be our main emphasis. It occurs as an outcome of some situation, issue or person.

We must be no longer attached, connected or concerned about the outcome of an issue or situation, particularly when we really have no control over that outcome.

It doesn't mean, however, that we don't care—quite the contrary, we may care a great deal. And caring doesn't necessary mean we are attached. The difference is that we just don't allow ourselves to try to take on another person's responsibility for some situation. Why? Because it is not ours to "attach to" in the first place, and we have no control of the outcome.

By allowing the mindset of non-attachment, we no longer have feelings or any vested interest regarding the outcome of the situation or issues another person is facing. Thus we can be free from stress or internal agitation.

When we attempt to take on another person's situation, or issues, what part of our being has gotten involved? Do you think the ego might like some type of involvement? Absolutely!

The ego likes to conjure up some expectations to that outcome. Whether the ego feels justified—or, more likely, simply does not accept that its attachment is unjustified!

Do you really think there is any justification when the ego is in control? I can't think of any cases that truly are justified; it's just the ego attempting to run the show, and exercise some control over another person or situation.

It would be important then to remember that another person's issues are their own—*not yours!* They, whether they realize it or not, ultimately have the needed answers within themselves. And we might be able to assist by just allowing the process to unfold naturally, versus trying to force some outcome. Sometimes it's like peeling an onion, one layer at a time. Be patient, and allow your compassionate listening to be of comfort.

Your lovingly offered listening can be an incredible gift to the other person. Perhaps the wisest path to take is that of solely a listener or an observer. Offering advice can change the dynamics between the two individuals. Can you offer suggestions? My question to you is: Can you offer any suggestions lovingly without any attachment?

Now, how could attachments start? It could be because we, as humans, want to be problem solvers. This problem solving could be either with other people's issues or the other people themselves. That is, of course, our own view, not that of the person going through a situation. I dislike using the word "problems" and prefer the words "issues about situations."

One area where I believe we have the potential to enter a no-win situation is with the mindset that when some advice is given then something is due in return or even expected or demanded.

When offering help, be very mindful of what you are doing, because it will always be from your own perspective, it can't possibly be from theirs. I also believe that when someone has a strong attachment to their own advice and they are demanding certain results, it is because they have an agenda of some sort and, certainly, an attachment.

Keep in mind that, if you are the recipient, the advice could be coming from a place other than love and peacefulness, perhaps the person is operating at the other end of the peacefulness spectrum, and might even be angry over your not following their suggestions.

Whatever it is, it is their issue, not yours, unless you also have decided to attach or embrace this situation.

Another thing to be aware of is that this "attachment" can be on the part of the person going through various issues and can also be on the part of the person offering assistance. Be aware!

A person might have some degree of expectation going forward. Have you ever heard someone say "that person better not disappoint me," or worse yet, "that person better not disappoint me again"? In the latter case, the use of the word "again," might give the impression that someone is carrying unnecessary, past, negative baggage. Elevating anything negative from the past into the present is asking for trouble.

Anyone adding past issues has a slim chance of being satisfied about present issues, and may produce pain and/or suffering, internally or externally. Why would anyone want or make this type of choice for their life?

Allow me to explain attachment and non-attachment by an example or two.

Let's say, you give a family member, some advice, either requested or unsolicited. First off, unsolicited advice could produce other than good results so try to stay away from this arena.

It is very important to keep in mind, when giving advice, *never* to do it in an attempt to manipulate or control the other person. That would be a prime example of having an attachment. Why? Because it's a no-win situation. There is an expression, "Always come from LOVE."

Okay, so you've given this person the best advice that you know and you *believe* you were "coming from LOVE." Now comes the rub—they didn't act on your advice.

You may think "How could they be so blind?" not to see the wonderful merits of this wisdom. You're now upset because they didn't actually use your insightful advice.

Let's look at the dynamics here. You are the giver of the advice and now you are upset or disturbed—you get my point, only you can best describe your feeling.

You had an ATTACHMENT. You really had an attachment! The ego, as in your ego, has just entered the picture. It wants control and has an insatiable appetite.

I might add that the ego is always willing to jump right into any situation in a heartbeat. How could they do that to ME? Well, they didn't do anything to you; you did this leap of ego, in your own mind, all by yourself. Who took this situation personally? You did, because of your attachment to an outcome.

Perhaps the next step is you'll even let yourself feel bad, certainly you're now off your state of peace. Further, do you realize that another person can never hurt your feelings, only you can do that by taking on what you perceive as their feelings toward you! The feelings we experience are and have always have been only our own feelings.

You can never feel other people's feelings, although you can experience similar life events. This is where compassion enters a situation. The only feelings you can ever have are those of our own! One of the ego's traps might look like what's discussed in the chapter "Someone Hurt My Feelings."

Sometimes in relationships the attachments can take on several different forms, one of which could be the dreaded "keeping score." When this occurs, no one wins, everyone loses. It is unwise to bring past events like that into the present, as they have nothing positive to offer in any situation. And this entire folly happened or started with someone wanting to bring the past into the NOW.

Let me list potential reasons why the advice given wasn't embraced, and see whether you may be able to add some of your own.

#1—The advice might have been viewed as wrong, and could not have worked for the person at this time in their life.

#2—Perhaps they weren't really ready to be a receiver (weren't open), and therefore it couldn't have worked for them. Unsolicited!

#3—They weren't listening.

#4—They could not see the solution in their mind's eye.

#5—The advice was unsolicited and unwanted. Watch out for giving unsolicited advice. In this case you were preaching, and no one was listening, or even wanted to listen to your self-imposed knowledge.

When a lesson is to be taught or advice given, and YOU are to be the teacher, you will be ready and prepared with exactly the right words of wisdom, for those truly in need. It is also wise to remember that "When the student is ready, the teacher will be there." Then you will have an opportunity to present a possible solution that may be needed for that individual (the student) at this time in their life.

Another saying is "Trust the process." As we travel through life we are all either students or teachers, and these roles can change in a heart-beat depending on the situation.

Wisdom can be found in the young as well as in elders and all those in between. Do not limit your inflow of knowledge to any particular age group, as life's answers are available to us in some unlikely places. I have found that I can learn from my grandchildren, if I will really listen to their pearls of wisdom. Wisdom is not age-bound! It is only found with our eyes, ears and hearts open.

Now let's look at the next example—not being attached to an outcome, thus non-attachment. Just for a moment, think how differently you would feel it you just gave this wise insightful information (wisdom) and then let it go and had no attachment.

That way, the person you are speaking to—the receiver—can come to their own conclusion. And you, the giver of advice, don't feel any unrest, or stress because you're *not* attached to the outcome. No one is feeling any pressure at any level. Sounds like a win-win situation.

Let's say, one of your children (older child, out of high school) asked for advice. First, make sure *you listen very closely* to what is being requested, looking for the requester's feelings.

Always take a few moments to consider your potential answer. Also consider whether an answer from you is really necessary at all! A quick response is an indication that little if any heartfelt thought went into your answer.

Ponder your answer, don't answer too quickly, and be honest, always keeping the requester's best interest at heart. Sometimes the best answer is to just listen.

Say you've listened, thought about your response, and considered your honest answer. Now it's time to deliver that answer. Consider telling the person that this is only your view (your perception) and is just one of the potential answers.

I cannot stress enough how important it is to let the other person know that it is *only your* point of view (perception) and there are or may be other answers to consider. This will give the receiver some latitude in understanding and being able to ask for additional information. Furthermore, it is also important to realize that the receiving person is hearing and internalizing this information from their perspective. Perhaps your answer warrants some deeper explanation.

Give the receiving person time to think about what you have said. If they seem perplexed you can ask if they have any questions or if you should explain further. If so, give your additional explanation; just remember to stay on track. Your answer is for and about the other person, *not you*.

Once this is done, now you *let go*, hence you have non-attachment. Another suggestion, when in doubt about how the information was received, ask them, "what did you hear?" This can be a huge enlightening key for both or all people involved, as it increases understanding and communication. That is what this is all about, effective communication and better understanding. As we work to better understand ourselves we also can better understand those we interface with in this world.

Once my oldest son, David, came to me with questions about a potential job change he was considering. We both are professionals but in entirely different disciplines. When he asked my advice, I realized a couple of things:

1. I was pleased that he came to me and asked my advice, which always makes a mom or dad feel very good inside.
2. I really didn't have a clue or any insight to give him for his field of endeavor.

So here was my reply: "Son, you have worked in your chosen field for several years, and you know far more than I would ever know about your field. With saying that, remember you have come to this point of considering change for some valid reason and you will make the right decision for yourself and your family's future.

"If, however, this decision doesn't seem right two weeks from now, or three years from now, any point in the future, you have the ability to re-choose. I will support you in any way that I can as you move forward in your life."

Giving him this answer felt good, and I knew it was the proper answer. As for me, what did I learn? In a word—a lot! This was an "ah ha" point in my personal growth, and I am thankful.

This doesn't mean you should or I should go around either giving unsolicited advice or restricting wise council, but we must be aware of their request or non-request. A person would be wise to know that unsolicited advice may be a request for *no* advice.

Monks from parts of India, as well as other parts of the world, believe that when a person honestly asks a question with an Open Heart, if the listener has an answer, it is their duty to give that answer (information). Giving the information without any expectations or conditions attached.

It is also believed that a person cannot possess anything forever, and that the blessing is in giving of yourself and your knowledge to those in need. We have all entered this world without anything and that is exactly how we shall also leave it. We cannot hold information exclusively forever; it is not in our being. Only those who are foolish would believe they can possess or suppress anything forever.

Here we can see the Flow of Life's Energy;

it should not and cannot be concealed or kept hidden, because it can't be bound anyway or anyhow.

This energy, this wisdom, is part of the universe, it is not ours to own or hold, it is only ours to discover and share.

How many times have we noticed the difference in our feelings when we give information "with" and "without" attachment! The difference between those two states is either being in a state of peacefulness and grace or experiencing internal turmoil, unrest and self-induced stress. Which would you choose?

We may also remember that we all are of choice and can re-choose.

For me, it comes down to how my heart feels, for it is my best indicator. With my heart open and loving I feel wonderful, then everything is an indicator for me to pay closer attention to, as I move through life, for all it has to offer.

Personal notes...

Personal notes...

Non-Judgment or Judgment

The word judgment means to assess and assign value to something or someone. Judgment also could place a meaning of right or wrong, good or bad. Passing such judgments could be traps of the ego. Therefore, there could be comfort in *not* making any judgments.

When we can look at a person or a situation and, by not making a judgment, we allow it to just be as it is, nothing more nothing less. When the ego gets involved it can play the judgment game, passing a sentence or passing judgment for actions, situations or issues.

Of course that scene plays out in our mind, where we imagine that we are in total control; remember that total control can be only of ourselves, no one else. Yet some don't really understand that they can never be in total control over another person, and that in actuality to judge can be a fruitless action.

The judgment I'm talking about here is not the type against mankind, the state, the nation or the world. It is on a far more personal level. The Bible makes several references to judgment and non-judgment.

Consider this thought regarding non-judgment: When one person feels they are not being judged by another person they are willing to share more of themselves. The so-called walls are removed or at least lowered. Now both people have an opportunity to learn even more about each other as well as about themselves. Because this new and different energy always flows toward and from both individuals!

There could be a whole slew of reasons why a person may want to judge another; one example could be that it results from fear. Let's take a moment and look at why fear may have entered this situation.

Sometimes it seems very obvious and at other times it's very well hidden. If fear could be an object, then what would it look like? How would it impact the situation? Fear could be the reason of putting someone, or some group down, seeking to elevate your own personal agenda.

When one person judges another, they have a tendency to place themselves either above that person or below them. Therefore it would be to our advantage to aspire to a state of not passing any judgment, that of non-judgment.

Let's look at some of the things that might happen when a person goes "to judgment," as in the above case. If a person puts themselves above the other person, from their point of view they are better (superior) than the other person, and may think the other person isn't trying hard enough, lacks the skills or lacks the desire to elevate themselves, from one level to a higher level.

Could fear have entered this scenario? Yes, although it may not be apparent! Then the ego might jump in and plant the seed that says, "What happens if they rise above me?" This could be the next slant of the ego's follies. Now fear has set in and worry about the unknown starts to flourish.

This is not a good situation, and the ego is on a roll. The next thought might be something like, "If they achieve a higher level than me, I could really feel threatened, in my job or personal environment."

So we can see that the ego has an opportunity to work in either direction, always enjoying working overtime. In either extreme, the results are not gratifying. The feeling of superiority moves us to insecurity and fear of losing what we believe we have. On the other end of the spectrum we may have feelings of despair; again this could move us to insecurity and fear.

One is a feeling of being superior; the other is a sense of lack or emptiness. With the ego in control there is really a no-win situation.

Franklin D. Roosevelt said, "All we have to fear is fear itself." Is fear a projection of the ego? My answer would be a resounding yes. Awareness of this fact is a wonderful tool to be used and remembered for now and in the future.

When we judge, we make a selection, which holds us back from our truest and perhaps best potential outcome. It also closes off some seen or unseen opportunities. Will we always find ourselves at some point of making a selection? Yes, there is a difference in making a judgment and simply making a selection. Is selecting food or a style of clothing a selection or a judgment?

Let's take a moment to look deeper at these two different examples. Food—selection or judgment? Answer—yes and yes. You may ask how this could be both. You select a certain food, it could be for taste, as a comfort food or for some other reason, and thus you might say this is definitely a selection.

How about if you choose the food because it is better for your long-term health, or it promotes the dietary goals you want to achieve. Now that could be viewed as a judgment, because you went out of your way to preserve or promote your health.

Both of these were done within your own mind. A similar argument could be made regarding clothing; is it for style, looks, comfort, projection of image, etc. I'm sure you get my point.

Let me tell you a personal story about food where it is being a selection and judgment as well as good and bad. Let's say I decide to order a pizza. I like pizza, so this was easy.

Was that a good selection of a bad selection? We'll see as the example unfolds. Size: large, medium or small, I choose medium. Best choice for me is always small, you'll see why. I go with medium because then I can have leftovers for the next day. Notice I didn't say half the pizza for the next day. Because I didn't want to limit myself! For me pizza is a comfort food.

Now I take it home and start consuming it while watching a movie.

Then, I notice that I've eaten one slice less than half—hey, I'm doing well. Although the movie I'm watching is only about half over. So I slowly and continually eat more pizza. Hey, I'm getting full, I have to slow down. In the end there is only one slice left for tomorrow.

Okay, where are the good and the bad in these decisions/judgments? The good: it's yummy. Now the other-than-good, so call them bad: I ate way too much, felt uncomfortable and lost my self control. I'll bet you didn't know pizza could do all those things. One last bad point, this eating usually happens well after 8 P.M. for me, so I go to bed plump. Plump is such a descriptive word.

Let's review my case with pizza; selection or judgment? Good or bad? It was selected out of craving (usually not a good move), therefore a bad judgment on my part. It's a comfort food for me, again usually not my brightest move. So I could also say poor judgment. Okay, okay, bad judgment.

My pizza consumption: I had good intent although it yielded bad results for me. Have I learned from past experiences? Well maybe yes, maybe no. And all this went on in my own mind, so think of all the opportunities you potentially may have before you. This is both a simple and silly use of something as easy as food as an example.

Other issues or situations have far different results, not only for you yourself, but for others as well.

Going back to judgment, in and of itself it could hold us back from a more peaceful, gentle, loving life, which most of us desire and deserve. And this all started because of the thoughts in our minds. The mind is extremely powerful.

Now, because of increasing our awareness, we are aware of our personal judgments. Not all judgments have lasting effects in our lives. And I am not suggesting you be critical of all judgments, just be aware of whatever you consider important. What can we do next? Don't judge!

Awareness is a very important KEY to happiness and peacefulness in our lives.

Without awareness, we could be like "electric bumper cars" bumping around the track at the carnival. Oh boy, now I've dated myself. If you don't know what electric bumper cars are ask you parents and hopefully not your grandparents.

If you have to ask your grandparents, I'm really old. Enough of that!

Awareness is our ability to intuitively differentiate internally right from wrong; and this can be seated in our core being. Boy did I really say right and wrong? Awareness can also come from family and loved ones, friends, colleagues, co-workers—any number of sources.

Oh, yes, also from personal experiences. Sometimes those are the most meaningful and the results can be longer lasting.

If we also learn from what others have experienced, perhaps we won't have to re-trace some of their uncomfortable experiences. Wouldn't we all like that better? I know some things I would rather not have experienced first hand!

Okay, now let's say that we are all aware, and with our awareness we can watch for ourselves starting to make judgments for any number of reasons. And with this awareness, we can choose not to make any judgment, or we can jump right in with both feet and judge.

Yes, we could stop and re-choose not to make a judgment. This would be an act of non-judgment. Non-judgment can only be accessed through and because of our awareness. Another thought: judgment usually has some sort of attachment, so be aware.

Like *attachments*, judgments can be personal ego traps. So, now that you realize you have a choice, release yourself and DON'T make or have any (or perhaps fewer) attachments or judgments. Of course, you might say, easy for you.

Practice, practice, practice is the way to start working on the "non's," so choose something small and easy, when something arises.

Another bit of information: the level of difficulty is of our choosing. Now that is a statement a lot of people choose not to embrace as a belief.

Make it mildly difficult—or easy, or make it very difficult, it's your choice. These decisions you are making are really personal choices. And if one situation seems too difficult, choose something a little easier, as a first adventure.

Another point about the difficulty level: it can be our own personal perception. So ask your higher power for or pray for a different perception. It certainly can't hurt, can it?

Sometimes when a judgment is made it can affect our personality, affect us mentally and physically, and not necessarily in a positive fashion. So why would we do that to ourselves?

Some judgments/decisions, in my humble view, could affect our health, either short-term or long-term. I'm very protective of my health and will do all that I can to maintain a healthy lifestyle. I do have my weaknesses, as explained in the pizza adventure.

Do keep in mind that some simple decisions can have very long-term effects. Are we looking at the positive or good changes/decisions/judgments we select to make for ourselves and our lives? Because they can also affect others in our lives, so again be aware!

I'd like to tell you an old story/folktale about a farmer and his friend, the villager. The fable is worth considering when making any judgments about a situation and its outcome. As you will see, sometimes a judgment can be premature and could also have been an incorrect conclusion at the time.

Here's the story roughly as it has been passed on to me. The setting is in a small village in a farming community in a small European country. In times of old there was a villager who went to visit his friend the farmer daily.

On one such visit the villager said to the farmer, "How lucky you are to have such a wonderful and strong horse to work your fields." To which the farmer replied, "Maybe yes, maybe no."

The next day when the villager came to visit the farmer he learned that the horse had run away. To this the villager replied, "How sad you must be to have lost your wonderful strong horse." Again the farmer replied, "Maybe yes, maybe no."

The following day, on the villager's visit he saw that the horse had returned with a herd of wild horses, and the villager said, "How fortunate you are to now have so many horses." Again the farmer replied, "Maybe yes, maybe no."

The next day the farmer's son was in the process of breaking one of these wild horses, and was thrown from the horse and broke his leg. The villager, upon hearing this news, said, "How sad, now your son will not be able to work in the fields or help around the farm." Again the farmer replied, "Maybe yes, maybe no."

Now, in this country where the farmer and villager lived, there was some battling with a neighboring country and their country's army was gathering up all available young men to fight. When the army came through and saw that this young man had a broken leg, thus they could not use him, they dismissed him from service and let him stay on the farm. When the villager received word of how the farmer's son was to stay on the farm, he was elated. He rushed to the farmer to share his joy and happiness with and for the farmer and his son. To this the farmer said, "Maybe yes, maybe no...."

So perhaps the message here is to remain constant, stay in the moment and don't make any judgments, as we probably don't really know the extent of the outcome.

We may not know the extent of our blessings, or even see them as blessings. Therefore perhaps time and patience are required, so be easy and gentle with yourself as well as with others. Allow time for things to unfold. Life at times will offer challenges and we may not see the blessing for some time to come. It sure doesn't mean they are not there; they are just unseen at the present moment.

Life is a process that is continually unfolding with hope, faith and the blessing of non-intervention. Do you think you control your life? Well, think again! At best you can control your judgments, so judge wisely! Life is not to be controlled anyway; it is to be lived and, we hope, enjoyed.

We are all on our own personal journeys in this life, and the more we practice the better we will become at observing and making better choices. Another word for "choice" could be judgment or non-judgment.

For me, the best way to be aware is to act as my own observer. It's like being a watcher of my own actions, like stepping outside my "self." And, yes, there are books that address this "stepping outside oneself" phenomenon or being an observer of oneself.

I can achieve an incredible amount of freedom in my own mind and well-being by not judging or passing judgment on other people or situations. Being patient and allowing some situations to unfold in their natural order.

This natural order is something of which I have no control, nor would I desire to have any control in the first place. This could also be described as: trusting the process. And it always works best without judgment!

Personal notes...

Personal notes...

Living Your Dreams

What in the world does that mean anyway? It's about having a dream and following "it" until "it" has been realized.

What are your dreams or visions? When you do start to realize that your dreams or visions control your perceptions, and that your perceptions become your reality.

It's also important to understand that your dreams or visions must have purpose and passion. When the dream or vision is clear, the creativity of that dream is clear as well. It is the light that shines within us, that illuminates our dreams. This all happens when we trust ourselves enough to let our dream out.

How do you accomplish such a task? Once

the dream has been born and thought about regularly, you can then start to make decisions that support it. This requires a constant vigil and focus. Because you must make decisions every day that do support your dreams.

In the process you'll be living your dreams on the journey toward the realization of them. Because this is not just about the destination alone—it's about the journey or process in accomplishing your dreams.

This process goes on forever until you accomplish your dream or you have decided to give up the dream. Is it wrong to give up your dream? Only you can answer that question.

If we look back in time we'll see that a lot of great people were in fact living their dreams. We could look to Thomas Edison and the electric light bulb, or the Wright Brothers and the aeroplane.

Orville and Wilbur Wright dreamed of a flying machine that could take off and land under its own power and control. They started by studying the flight of various birds, and also studied the designs of gliders from some of their contemporaries, and experimented over and over again.

They were constantly making changes and

modifications. There were challenges and set-backs, although they kept their dream alive and continued to focus on the outcome of flying.

Today some may say that is a waste of time, that you're being a silly dreamer. Who has the power to destroy another's dreams? How many times have we heard the words "you can't do that," or even spoken them?

Yet others may offer more constructive comments like, "How can I live my dream?" or "How can I help you live your dream?"

Well there are a number of ways:

1st—Believe in your dream.
2nd—Make decisions that support your dream.
3rd—Have confidence in yourself that you can live your dream.
4th—Most importantly—Don't buy into the belief when others tell you that you can't accomplish your dreams.

Because it's about doing what is necessary to accomplish your dreams or goals. Don't sabotage yourself or let someone else sabotage your dreams.

My son Paul had a dream, which started in his teen years, of being in the music industry, "the business," as Paul would say. Well at least that's Dad's interpretation of his dream. He worked hard, did his research and continued to follow his heart's desire. There were challenges as well as folks who said he didn't have the talent to accomplish such a task. That he was wasting his time.

With his tenacity and perseverance, he is now living his dream. And yet he still feels he has a way to go, therefore he continues to focus on his dream.

Again, the dream is about the journey or process. Paul is on his journey and making decisions that support his dream.

What's important to realize is that the dream isn't the destination, but living the dream really is about the journey or process towards accomplishment for each of us individually.

If we look at our own lives, there have been times we have had dreams—and we've lived them! Hopefully we realized what was happening, although a lot of times it is so natural it could go unnoticed.

Let me use an example: a thought came to you and you decided it was something you wanted. Then you started doing what was necessary to accomplish your dream or desire.

These could be simply helping someone,

getting something, doing something; whatever it was, it started out as a *thought* and turned into a *dream*.

When we realize we're living our dreams, it is absolutely wonderful. Different feelings can arise during these times, like euphoria, calmness, peacefulness, just to name a few. Then again we may have had dreams that we didn't accomplish! Why do you think that could have happened? Perhaps we let the dreams drift away or even die.

A person might say, "I could never live my dream!" Why is that? It could be because the dream wasn't strong enough or the commitment to the dream wasn't strong enough.

So ask yourself, do you believe in yourself, do you believe in your dream? Or are you just selling yourself short or selling yourself out?

Perhaps you believe what others are telling you about YOUR DREAM. How could another person know your true potential! They can't!

If you're having difficulties focusing on your dreams, perhaps they've started off a bit lofty. Remember if you can't see yourself accomplishing your dream or goal, you won't.

Whatever you decide *you're* RIGHT—if you say you can do it *you're right*, if you say you can't *you're right*. Only you process this power for yourself and your dreams.

In the process of living your dreams, as your confidence grows, so will your accomplishments. The joy you will experience can be life-changing for yourself as well as those around you. Start *living your dreams*, right now, this day, this instant.

*P*ersonal notes...

Personal notes...

Tune In &
Tune Up

At first glance, the title might make you may wonder what this chapter is about. Well, it's not about *tuning in* to a radio station or a TV program. Also it's not about getting a *tune up* for your car.

It's far more personal. Initially I had thoughts of illustrating this concept by comparing myself and another person. But the more I thought about this approach, the more I realized that the process is really only about self. And how we can better be aware of our own state of being, as well as tuning in more often to what is really going on within ourselves. After first looking at the aspects of tuning in, we will then look at tuning up.

When you think about tuning in to yourself, what do you imagine is involved? In a word: awareness! Sometimes a person could look at a situation and say, "I wasn't even aware that was happening." Perhaps we were oblivious to the issues at that time.

To tune in is to be aware or conscious of the present moment. Remember that awareness and consciousness go hand in hand. Therefore as we become more aware of what is really going on within ourselves, then our consciousness level can and will be raised.

We will start to become observers of our own selves, what we're doing as well as saying and thinking.

So this is really about you for yourself, as it is about me for myself. When we move to include other people, we tend to form judgments and/or may feel we have the answers for their particular situation or sets of issues. These, by the way, are ego issues. What compels us to judge others? (I discuss my thoughts on that subject in the chapter on non-judgment.)

There is, however, another aspect of judgment to be aware of, and that is self-judgment. Is self-judgment good or bad? It depends on what we do with that judgment, so for now just be aware when you are judging yourself.

Another point is that of responsibility. Being unaware does not alleviate our responsibility. It might, however, make it more difficult to recognize.

Going around with our heads in the clouds doesn't mean that there isn't any ground below us. Also, if our heads are in the sand it doesn't mean that there is no sky above us. Don't go to either extreme.

If a person were to jump off an elevated position, they might even enjoy the falling (or perhaps the flying) part of this adventure; the disturbing part is the results of the landing. Ouch!

As my nephew liked to say to his kids when they were growing up: "There are always consequences for your action." So consider your choices!

Let's also look at the thoughts we might have in regard to our responsibility. Who is responsible for our personal thoughts? You're right—*you* are! For every thought that is held in our minds, we potentially began a process of manifestation, to create a particular situation, which matches what we hold as our perception.

In words from the *Course in Miracles*, "I

will be accountable for how my day is going" (that is, your own thoughts and perceptions). "If I don't like how that feels, it's up to me to monitor my thoughts and change them." There is a little saying that goes along with this train of thought: "What you perceive you receive."

Now let's look at what happens when we expand our awareness to include another or others. What effect can be derived? How can we be of assistance to those in a state of un-awareness? Or can we really help anyone? It depends; maybe yes, maybe no. Because this is ultimately up to the other individual, not you. It is for their needs, and should be their responsibility or ability to recognize their position in any situation.

When another person is ready to learn, they will see answers (or solutions) to their lesson or lessons. Remember that, like ourselves, all their answers are within themselves and will be revealed to them at the right and proper time.

So can we really help? Yes, perhaps by holding gentle loving thoughts within our minds and praying for the particular individual. When the answers are revealed to them, you can help by showing them your loving manner so they can find peace and resolution for a particular issue or situation.

egarding any suggestions you offer, maybe you should also ask yourself: is this something that another person may need; or is it really something I need? Then you may realize that this is a lesson for you yourself! You might remember this saying, "If you spot it—you got it."

Therefore it may really be about you and not the other person. With your awareness you can acknowledge, bless it and let it go.

Perhaps this lesson was really sent for you. And you were lucky enough to recognize it in someone else. A person may say "Don't shoot the messenger"; in this case the messenger is delivering for *you*! Once you have observed this lesson, and realize it is one of your *own* lessons to be learned, be grateful.

Okay, you have a negative thought, and for whatever reason you decide to latch onto this particular thought. Wow, and you now decide to believe this thought. Why would you attach to a negative thought? Simple answer, because you are of choice. A point to remember: you can re-choose.

Now you run with this thought and start to embrace it as true or actually real. Boy, that could be scary—not to mention the potential consequences. Sometimes the first clue is how you feel, and generally it isn't good.

How do we notice or become aware? It's by our ability to sense that we are off our peace, or no longer in a state of peacefulness. By the way, you'll know it intuitively, that is, if you haven't become numb to the body's messages.

Which takes us to the study of kinesiology, wherein it's accepted that the body doesn't lie. The challenge is for us is to recognize any slight change in our body's internal environment or temperament. Whatever it was that gave us this uncomfortable feeling was sensed by our internal feedback mechanism.

We all have this mechanism; it is, however, up to us to see its messages. Those are the "red flags" that pop up from time to time. Should you ignore these "red flags"? Well, should you ignore a heart condition? Awareness—do you think it might be important? Once aware, now you have to decide which path you will choose.

What could happen when someone chooses *not* to listen, or see the signals of the inner feeling or inner voice, that quiet voice that guides us on this journey through life? Why would a person ignore the inner voice, or inner sense?

Perhaps because we have allowed ourselves to become numb. Such numbness may start with the thought that says: "Don't let that little thing bother you, it will go away." So this gentle and loving inner voice gets pushed deeper and deeper within us until we can't hear it any longer. Then later we may not even recognize that we have such an inner voice.

When we quiet ourselves from the mind's chatter or the busyness that bombards us constantly, we allow or give ourselves over to an opportunity to elevate to a higher level of awareness. This is when we can enter our own sanctuary, and perhaps hear this inner voice.

It's been said that when our spirit is speaking to us, it is the voice of God. And it will speak to us only when it is invited. How do we invite this inner voice to speak to us? It might be through listening and through our ability to be quiet and patiently wait for the answers that will come.

Here we have an opportunity to take a walk of faith; "Have faith and you shall receive." Keep in mind that there is also another voice that likes to grab our attention by its noisiness and controlling nature. That, my friends, is the voice of the ego. It hates this quietness as well as our internal peacefulness.

When I am in this state of peacefulness, I

feel so at ease and I am grateful. For I am full of love, joy, and happiness. It is through this peacefulness that I can now send positive energy out to others throughout the entire world.

Keep in mind that this is a place I can go whenever I choose. Or when I feel it's necessary for my own well-being and spiritual good. It is essentially taking care of myself.

Another important point to remember is that we all have this quiet sanctuary within. You may find that hard to believe, although it is absolutely true. Therefore it may be your challenge and opportunity to find your path to go there, because no one can find it for you.

Once this peacefulness has been experienced, we can also recognize its splendor and its unbounded positive loving energy. And we can go to this peaceful sanctuary at any time of our choosing.

Yes, it is only the busy mind, which is loud and noisy, that restricts us from even seeing such a place.

How can we find such a quite place? As I have alluded to earlier, meditation may be one way.

Another suggestion would be to concentrate on your breathing. With an exercise of deep breaths, in through your nose, out though your mouth. Do it several times and concentrate, think of nothing else except your breathing. This exercise can have a very calming effect. Have you ever been in a pine forest? Let's say you were to find yourself in a pine forest and, as you quieted your busy mind, then you might be able to really hear the whispering of the "whispering pines."

Ultimately what we want is to tone down the noise (reduce the volume) of the mind. Our minds are continuously churning, and one of the things that most of us do is to attach to various passing thoughts during this bombardment.

Well, how about not doing any attachments to any thoughts! How do we do that? By just acknowledging then letting the thoughts go. Believe me, it takes practice and more practice.

When a person feels stuck in some situation, why would they choose to stay stuck? Perhaps, it's comfortable, something within their comfort zone, or it's what they're used to.

If that's really the answer, and you ask "Why is it comfortable?" the response could be, in a word, "fear." Fear of what?—how about the unknown!

Sometimes being stuck seems okay because

it's familiar and the person may be unaware they may have another choice or option. Then how could help be obtained? (Keep in mind this person could well be yourself.)

The most basic answer is by offering love. Is there anything better than offering love without expectations? This can be a challenging task, especially if we are in a close relationship with this person. If the person is ourselves, then of course we have a personal relationship. And this can be the most challenging.

Sometimes that personal relationship helps to "muddy up" the waters of clear thinking and resolve. Especially when it's ourselves, because we may want to stay in a state of un-forgiving-ness of ourselves.

A positive response could be to hold only loving thoughts for ourselves or the other person. Don't be afraid to share your feelings, unless you are uncomfortable.

Although, if you would rather not verbalize, there is real power by just saying "I love you" to yourself, silently and repeatedly when with the other person. This could even work for yourself. It's a re-enforcement of spirit.

There are times when words may help and times when your silence can speak volumes.

When someone knows within their heart that you will do what is necessary, with your heart open and ready to be of assistance on their personal life's lessons, they will be grateful. They will in turn have an opportunity to be more open and receptive to offering kindness and love to others.

It's the quietness of the mind that is the most revealing and healing. This quietness of our minds can truly be sensed by others. It shows in the positive energy we exude.

Could the sticking point be the ego, is the ego that powerful? Absolutely! Where does the ego get its power? It comes from us personally, because we allowed or gave our power over to the ego.

This significant realization can be life-altering, depending how we understand and address various issues. Let's say we have a negative thought and we embrace it. Perhaps then we have offered this thought a life of its own, unbeknownst to ourselves. We may even feel it has become one of our own personal stories, "a drama."

Thus we have relinquished our power to the ego and allowed it to embark on whatever path it chooses to travel. A lot of times that's one of drama, and so easily bought into because most folks like dramas.

Why is that such an easy choice? Because in our worlds of drama, we are in control or at least we allow for the illusion of control. Buying into this control fantasy can be alluring. Also the ego is a lot louder, in our minds, than the peacefulness of the Holy Spirit that also resides quietly within. The ego wants to be *right* at any cost and control.

When we enter into a drama, we subject ourselves to the whims of the ego's directions and decisions. Thus we might feel we have no control whatsoever, maybe even the converse, and we begin to believe the illusion(s). We now feel we get to run the show, direct the movie, and be in control.

Hopefully we can see that there is falseness in such thinking, and offer up a chuckle. For the world doesn't really revolve around one person's expanded ego. Although we do get to run our own lives, where the problems arise is when we attempt to run the lives of others.

It would be very helpful to realize, or "become aware" of, our part in this situation or illusion. Once we become aware, then we can consider a wide range of different choices.

• • •

When a life comes into existence it is pure love, as is so noticeable in the smiles and giggles of babies and young people. Then at some point in time something changes and the ego starts to develop its separateness. The ego encourages and thrives on our separation, not connectedness, not togetherness and certainly not any type of oneness. It is opposed to such oneness, such as the "oneness with God."

Once we realize that we are all connected within this universe, we can then approach a lot of the situations in life with a different perspective. With the ego in control, it is looking to feel absolutely right. Would you rather be right or would you rather be peaceful? The answer should be self-evident.

There is a saying from a friend of mine, Toni, and I'm paraphrasing: "If you're absolutely certain, then you are absolutely blind." As the Bible says, "Let those who have eyes, see." It's far more important to be open, loving and aware than to be right!

Another passage from the Bible: "Love your brothers and sisters as you would love yourself." When our ego is on a rampage, it would lead us to believe that we ourselves are unlovable. Not only to ourselves, but also to everyone else.

What a sad set of thoughts to buy into or even believe! If we can't or won't allow love for ourselves then we can't offer love to anyone else. This line of thinking presents a lot of internal struggles, therefore don't believe this type of thinking. It has no value to you or anyone whose life you might touch.

Can we just become aware and re-choose? Where does awareness start to develop? It is found within the confines of the quietness of our inner self. And the answer is really our personal resolve or determination to choose peace, or to re-choose peace when we're having turmoil within our lives.

What is one of the easiest ways to invoke this quietness? The answer can be found in a single word: prayer. Why is it so powerful? It allows each one of us to enter this, our inner realm, in our own way. Therefore it is without any pressure and without any expectations.

When in a state of prayer, we allow a form of connectedness to a power far greater than our own individual selves. We could call this connectedness "the power of God," which is universal. Prayer isn't something to be is done only in church; it can be achieved and embraced moment to moment, anywhere, at any time.

• • •

A few years ago I was in the process of journaling morning pages and came to realize that journaling, for me, was a form of prayer. From this exercise, I began to realize that this writing was becoming my "prayer writing." I started to notice that these writings were more like something coming through me, than created by me.

I looked at what I had journaled and saw the following statement one day: "I Am holding the Blessed hand of God this Day—Moment to Moment."

This is when I realized that my journaling was opening an opportunity for me to be a conduit of positive energy, and it allowed me a connectedness to this higher power. Therefore what I was writing was actually coming through me as a connectedness to my higher source.

How did this affect me? It allowed me to look at my life's journey in a different aspect—journaling. When I think about these last few statements, I notice that journaling is just one of many forms for me to tap into or choose from in my life.

We can be and are all conduits for this wonderful flow of energy, if we are open and make ourselves available to it. Look at the word conduit—by definition, it is allowing something to pass through, unrestricted. Which goes back to non-resistance. If we are really conduits for life's energy, what happens when we choose to restrict this flow of energy?

Let's look at it this way, whenever we feel we can hold on to something, anything, we are being restrictive. By the act of sheer holding we can't receive whatever is coming next into our lives. Whatever is coming next can be either blessings, lessons or both. The key here for us to remember is that all lessons are blessings. Hence to see the blessings can at times be our real challenge!

Another major changing point in my life was accepting the idea of coming from gratitude. As in, adopting an "attitude of gratitude." You may ask, what does this mean or how do we "come from gratitude"? It's pretty simple, just be grateful for everything.

An easy place to start is being grateful for the fresh air we breathe, or even for being able to breathe. When a person begins the process of being grateful for all their surroundings it becomes very expansive very quickly, and this act is quite refreshing as well as rewarding.

Thus giving thanks *"for all that we are and all that we have,"* not using any of our valuable life's energy on thinking about the "lacks" of, or in, our lives. This is another form of awareness, and through increasing awareness we can make better choices and or re-choices. But if we choose to think about "lacks," we rob ourselves of the joy of a grateful heart.

Now let's talk about the *tune up* part of this chapter. What I mean by tune up is to *elevate* yourself, which is raising your awareness as well as your own consciousness. When we do this, we also have the ability to elevate those around us. By the positive energy field we are emanating outward. The lives we touch will also touch others, and so on and on.

At times we may find ourselves in down moods, and this can be understandable, but how we choose to deal with these down or lower-energy situations makes all the difference in our life and the lives of those we touch.

Perhaps you have heard of the mirror effect. Briefly, it's about the reflections of our lives, and it's our outward expression that is directly linked or "mirrored" to our inner life and what we hold as our attitude towards our own life.

What a person sees of our outside is directly a mirror of what is within us and how we view our lives internally. Can a person fool others with their outward appearances? Absolutely! Although, as we may have heard in the past, "no one can fool all the people all the time." It will take its toll.

When in a down mood, one of the things we can do for ourselves is to physically move. An example would be to move into the presence of others who have positive attitudes and good positive energy. Or even go for a walk, sit and listen to the birds, which I am doing right now on my deck.

Change your environment and thus the energy field that you are currently being exposed to. Good positive energy is contagious, thus you will absorb the essential energy of this new environment.

Also, when you're in a down or bad mood, talking might not be the wisest thing to do. Just being receptive and open could be enough. A few words about talking when in a down or bad mood: a closed mouth gathers NO feet.

Let me use our hands for this example: When you're holding onto a down mood you can't receive love in your hands. Remember that if your hands are holding something, anything, they can't be open to receive. Open your hands and open your heart and open your mind.

Another way to express the above point is that we are all an outward expression of our internal spiritual-self. And we all have this consciousness within, which is just waiting patiently to be discovered, known and embraced. We should let our light shine, for it is who we really are—be a light unto this world.

Here's a little exercise to try for a week or longer. Every morning upon waking, before you get out of bed, think of all the things you have to be grateful for in your life. It may start out as a short list of ten or twenty things, and in time will grow.

Be careful not to enter into or entertain negative thoughts or any thoughts of lack, or even of comparing yourself to others. For this type of negative mental review never builds an *uplifting* result. Think about all the good things you can truly be grateful for in your life. Before long you will notice more and more things for which to be grateful.

This exercise can and should continue after you're up and moving around in your daily life. Because you might find yourself in a challenging situation from time to time, and it doesn't mean that there isn't something you can sincerely be grateful for in this situation.

Don't ever hold back from offering up a silent prayer of gratitude. Once hooked on this little exercise, you will find it can give you peacefulness any time it's needed. Peacefulness is a state of mind and it always starts within our own selves.

How about this for a resolution when processing a negative thought: I must have decided wrongly because I am not at peace any longer. Always monitor and be aware of your thought, because that's where it all begins.

Can we raise ourselves to a level of love? Yes, absolutely, because love can vaporize or neutralize all the negative issues and irritations in our life. If you don't think that love could really help, try this exercise:

When at a point of perhaps anger with someone, try to stay in this state of anger while also offering unconditional love to that same person. It can't be done. So what is the answer?

Offer only love, and see how wonderfully that will affect your life and your personal well-being. Why? Because nothing else really matters at the end of the day, or certainly at the end of one's life.

You may ask, does faith have anything to do with tuning up? Absolutely! Without faith we can be lost on this journey of our life. What is faith?—it is the belief in the unknown or the unseen. When reading in the Bible, you see countless references to faith or to having faith. Think about it, what would our world look like without any faith?

As stated in the Bible, offering us a lesson about faith:

Be Still and Know that I Am.

Personal notes...

Personal notes...

Being of Choice

What is one of the biggest non-truths that a person might accept as a truth? The answer is "I don't have a choice." It's amazing how many people buy into this falsehood. Where does something like that even get started?

Someone might have said to you, "You don't have any choice!" Maybe this person was older and wiser (or at least perceived to be wiser) so you believed them.

It may have been years ago and you may still be holding on to that old belief. If that's the case, why? Maybe you're afraid to let go of this misguided belief. Again: Why? You really can re-choose. The worst thing that could happen is that, if you don't like what you have chosen, now you get to re-choose or maybe even re-choose again. A lot of times we may hear the excuse "I'm committed, so now I'm stuck, I simply can't change my decision." Well, that simply isn't true.

When you make a decision it's your choice. Remember, you are the person doing the choosing. That, by definition is "being of choice." If the particular choice isn't good for you, then you can re-choose. You may be thinking, I can't just re-choose. And why can't you re-choose?

Let's look at any situation where you made a decision and after some period of time you changed your mind. Now you may think, I can't just change my mind now, it's too late. You can always change your mind, always.

If you think that isn't true, guess what, politicians do it all the time. Sometimes they change their minds, positions or views within the same sentence!

A person can always re-choose, and in some cases that's the wisest action. Particularly when changing their decision is in the interest of safety. Another reason for changing their decision is that now they have additional information. Was re-choosing wise? Yes!

The thing to realize about choice is that

you always have a choice. Although there may be times when you feel you have no choice or control over your own life.

Keep in mind this is only from your personal perspective. When a person feels they have no control, power or responsibility in their life, what really needs to be understood is that they have total responsibility, power and control because they are of choice. Once this is understood, it becomes far easier to make decisions on the particular issue at that time.

Perhaps now you can begin to understand and accept your responsibility for your own choices. If you truly want something different in your life, choose differently! Remember we are 100% responsible for the choices we make! If you don't like the outcome—re-choose.

Don't be afraid to make a different or better choice. When something doesn't work out to our liking, we can be grateful for the lesson being offered to us, as well as accept the responsibility for the choices we have made. Now we can go back to the drawing board, so to speak, and look at different options, different choices.

Choices also give us opportunities to "try something on" and see how it feels. If it's not right for you, you can re-choose. When you make a choice, you have allowed yourself the ability to experience something, perhaps even new and different. Then you'll know for sure whether it's something you like or something you don't want to experience again.

Sometimes a person will put too much emphasis on a decision. Most of the decisions a person makes on a daily basis are not life-threatening. I'll bet you make multiple decisions each and every day, and you think nothing of those decisions because they have become routine.

As our lives evolve we will be given a lot of opportunities to make choices daily. Also when making a choice on something you are not sure of, you can always ask questions, and with better understanding you'll make better choices.

It's always wiser to make a choice when understanding your options or the ramifications of your choice(s). Although most decisions are on the casual side, some might be more serious and should receive deeper advance consideration.

When you think about it, re-choosing is always an option. This doesn't mean a person should go around making decisions and always changing their mind, particularly when other people are involved.

Being in service to others is a good choice. But be aware of self-serving motives. There is a difference between serving others and being self-serving.

When we make decisions we get to choose what we believe is best. Sometimes we may make decisions for ourselves alone, yet we should also remember we coexist on this planet; and some of our decisions could impact the lives of others. So be aware of the far-reaching implications of your decisions.

Let me share a couple of examples when making choices in restaurants. Have you ever felt you would rather have someone else select your meal for you? I go to a little restaurant near my home, called Stephano's. It's my "Cheers," you know "where everybody knows your name."

When I go there I generally ask Stephano what he would suggest for dinner, and then I go with his recommendation. Can I make my own decisions—yes of course! When I go there I'm open to his suggestions and he has never steered me wrong. You may think, oh Fred's just *lucky*. I, on the other hand, trust his judgment.

Another example can help show that there can be several reasons why a person might be reluctant to make a decision. One could be fear, as in fear of making the wrong choice. Let's say you arrive at a restaurant and are with a group of people, you've been seated, placed your orders, the meals arrive at the table and someone says, "Oh, your meal looks so much better than mine, I wish I had ordered what you have."

The best reply to give when that happens is simply say, "Next time you can." Or maybe they're a mini–meal-poacher and just want some of what you've ordered.

Basically what could have happened here is that the person didn't have a clue as to what they wanted to eat. Sometimes a person may feel rushed and will order what someone else ordered because it sounded good or even order by picture thinking "Boy, that looks good."

In defense of those who have difficulties making decisions (choices) at restaurants, sometimes it can be a challenge or even overwhelming. Particularly when the menu is huge with many different selections.

Have you ever gone to a restaurant for breakfast and been faced with a menu of sixty different choices? How many different ways can you make eggs or pancakes? Apparently a lot!

So far I've talked about making decisions, and that you can re-choose. Now there could be another side to situations, it's when you feel frozen about making choices, re-choosing or even feeling not at liberty to make any changes in your decision-making process.

So a person might start depending on others to make decisions for them. Is there anything wrong with that? No. Just so long that you realize that you are of choice, and you can make your own choices.

Letting someone else make decisions for you is a choice on your part. But there can also be the tendency to then become dependent or reliant on another's decisions.

Now when a person tells to you, "You don't have any choice" it's because they feel there are no other options for you. Well, guess what, you may have different ideas about your options.

It doesn't mean that the other person is wrong, they might believe they have the best option for you. Your decisions are always your own to make, not someone else's.

Our thoughts give us opportunities to make choices. Because with every thought we have two possibilities, either accept the thought and act on it or reject the thought and not act on it. If our thoughts come to us from our subconscious minds, then perhaps we may feel we have no control over those thoughts. Or do we? Once the thoughts become conscious to us then we have a choice to either act on them or let them pass.

The lives we are living now are a direct result of the decisions (choices) we have made throughout our lives. They have gotten us to this very point in time—right now!

The phase "I Can Choose Again" should become very present in your thinking, as you remember that every choice establishes your own identity, and you are the person who directly benefits from those choices.

Our lives can be living examples to others on how we have lived by our choices. Remember the choices we make will be noticed by others. If a change in your life seems necessary, that thought starts within your mind. Remember the only person you should really look at is yourself. For it is within you that you will find your answers.

Sometimes when you make a choice that you feel is right for you, others may attempt to sway your decision. This might be a time when you should reaffirm and re-enforce your commitment to your choice.

Another person's perspective will not match yours. And that's okay, because you have listened to their perspective. Now when a choice is made, your perspective comes into play; it's how we see things in our own lives. If the decision results in something we don't like, we can always re-choose.

When we realize that our perspective is governed by our thoughts, we see that by changing our thoughts, we're also changing our perspective.

Have you ever had a difference of opinion with another person? Of course you have, we all have. Since we can't change another person's mind or point of view, the only thing we can change is our own perspective.

Our view is fashioned by our thoughts of a particular situation. So if we want something different, we must choose a different thought pattern. Once this change happens, the circumstances within our lives could change to a more peaceful state.

It's the realization of thoughts that allows us to make different choices. Choices should be tailored more toward peaceful resolutions, as opposed to those which could have been made from some negative point of a view. Would you rather be right or at peace? It's your choice, and your first choice should always be peace.

How do we learn about making choices?

It's by our mistakes. From those mistakes we now have a better understanding of the ramifications of our choices. This will assist us in making better choices in the future.

When in doubt about a choice, quiet yourself and listen to the quiet voice within. That quiet voice is within each and every one of us. This voice will intuitively lead us in the right direction towards the answers we are seeking.

Here are some thoughts about choosing and being a victim. The person may be acting that way to draw attention to themselves or get another to agree with their feelings about their plight. Keep in mind this is only how they are viewing themselves at a particular moment in time. They can always re-choose, although most victims would not want to hear this when acting in that role. Sometimes re-choosing may seem difficult.

When a person is in the role of victim, they could be seeking or wanting more love in their life. Is it easy to make a choice to move in the direction of "LOVE"? Perhaps not, because the ego is always ready to be involved. The ego path may seem easier, or just easier to bear, yet these paths are all but peaceful.

Sometimes making a choice can be challenging, and we are really choosing whether to simplify or complicate our lives. Usually, simplifying is best. Why add unneeded stress? What good does it serve? If you came to the conclusion that it serves no one, you're right.

So, choices basically come down to two; we either offer love to someone or a situation, or we withhold love. Withholding love is what potentially holds us hostage away from our highest potential.

Looking at your state of peacefulness is a reflection on the choices you have made. The more you experience peacefulness, the more you'll be able to choose peacefulness over and over again.

This takes practice, but the more we focus on a state of peacefulness the less stress we'll experience in our lives. And we'll have the ability to return more and more easily to that state of peacefulness. It allows us to live more harmoniously with ourselves and others. The ego, however, would like to disrupt any state of peacefulness and offer agitation, confusion or anything to draw us off our peace.

When we are feeling under attack, remember: we have choices. We can engage (not necessary the wisest choice) or we can see past or through the current situation and seek a peaceful solution. Don't allow yourself to be drawn into this drama or situation, just act as an observer. This will allow you to think clearly.

In making a decision, be aware of your internal state of being! How you feel right now really matters. Have you ever noticed how comfortable you are at making choices when you are peaceful versus being agitated or upset?

Most people would like more peace in their lives; the challenge is to be aware and choose peaceful solutions, over and over again.

Sometimes people don't understand the anatomy of choices that are made day to day, moment to moment. Because now we can become monitors of our choices. This monitoring will intuitively show us when we are not at peace within ourselves.

Another useful point is that underneath all our decisions lies a belief and intention. So what do you believe and what do you intend? Knowing and understanding this provides a foundation for our choices and decisions.

At times we may feel bombarded by circumstances in our lives, which can be demanding our time and attentions, because we may feel a choice needs to be made right now. The challenge is to choose a peaceful solution.

If we do this, our lives can become over-all more peaceful. This does not mean that we won't have turmoil in our lives; it does, however, change how we view our own circumstances.

Therefore the lesson to take away is: we can re-choose. When we intuitively feel uncomfortable, that is the time to reevaluate the choices we have made and consider re-choosing a more peaceful alternative.

Personal notes...

*P*ersonal notes...